Breath of the Invisible

Breath of the Invisible
The Way of the Pipe
John Redtail Freesoul

This publication made possible with
the assistance of the Kern Foundation

The Theosophical Publishing House
Wheaton, Ill. U.S.A.
Madras, India / London, England

The Theosophical Publishing House
306 West Geneva Road
Wheaton, IL 60187

A publication of the Theosophical Publishing House,
a department of the Theosophical Society in America.

Library of Congress Cataloging in Publication Data

Freesoul, John Redtail.
    Breath of the invisible.

    (A Quest book)
    1. Indians of North America—Religion and myth-
ology.   2. Indians of North America—Medicine.
3. Indians of North America—Tobacco use.   I. Title.
E98.R3F74   1986   299'.7   86-40124
ISBN 0-8356-0611-2 (pbk.)

Printed in the United States of America

To

Trinity Freesoul
Helen Hardin
Albert and Rilla Tallbull
Alex and Annie Shoulderblade
Archie Blackowl
John (Fire) Lame Deer
Frank Fools Crow
Robert Swiftotter
Cynthia Shellwoman
Philip Deere
Richard Oakes
and the Cheyenne-Arapahoe Nation
(Author's royalties are donated to
Cheyenne orphans in Oklahoma)

About the Author

John Redtail Freesoul is a Cheyenne-Arapahoe artist, teacher, and professional therapist. For his distinguished artistry he has received twenty-seven awards including many first-place ribbons for ceremonial pipes awarded by the Southwestern Association on Indian Affairs.

John is the sacred pipeholder and spokesman for the Redtail Hawk Medicine Society. This is an intertribal society formed to be of service to the Elders and spiritual leaders of all tribes and to the revival of traditional Indian medicine for spiritual and therapeutic healing. Recently John was made the official pipemaker for the Cheyenne-Arapahoe tribes in Oklahoma.

Contents

Preface

I am not an authority on Indian medicine.
I am a servant to the medicine.
So be it.
In humility I speak.

Recently I entered into the autumn time in my life,
the position of the West on the Medicine Wheel. It
is a time of harvesting the lessons learned from experimenting and investigating ideas and experiences.
Growth and investigation continue, but the western
phase of a person's life involves slowing down and
deep introspection. Since my youth I have been
blessed with vivid spiritual visions, despite some of
my untamed ways. Sometimes I view myself as the
Great Spirit's prodigal son.

My spiritual vision and dream has been to write this
book, to share with you some of my life on the Red
Road of Earth Mother and Sky Father. I wrote also to
remind myself of the blessings of life. Some folks may
praise this book and others may criticize it. Few, I believe, will be the same after they read it, as I have read
it.

Another purpose in writing *Breath of the Invisible*
is to provide a workbook of exercises and a "field
guide." The role designations of instructor, shaman,
elder, healer, and medicine person are mentioned regularly, but you will notice the names of those folks
are seldom, if ever, mentioned. Nor is there a detailed
account of the dialogue between myself and my teachers, as appears in other books. Such is not included

out of respect. I believe that certain learning exchanges between student and teacher should remain intimate and private, although the lessons and realizations resulting from some exchanges may be, should be, shared to support the light of wisdom and higher consciousness.

I am experiencing a growing discontent with an escalating number of people who have found a medicine person willing to instruct them, yet are not satisfied to practice humbly and develop what they have learned. Instead they taint their experiences to develop exciting colorful stories and begin writing books. They may even travel as a self-proclaimed authority on Native American medicine. Their information is often inaccurate, sketchy, and grossly overgeneralized to apply to all Indian tribes, to all Indians everywhere.

It took me ten years of reflective prayer and of prodding close associates before I finally took pen in hand to write this book. Shortly after my fortieth birthday, I was instructed by a spirit guide in vision, during prayer and fasting, to document certain information about the sacred pipe and the Medicine Wheel. This does not make *Breath of the Invisible* better than other literature. My sharing of feelings on this issue is not a judgment of other statements; it is a testimony of my own inspiration. It is also a personal witness to you of what I perceive as a spreading and dangerous misuse and exploitation.

In some chapters there is repetition of what has already been mentioned. There is a reason. Some topics are incomplete. This is intentional to provoke your individual seeking and investigation. There is no other way to do this.

These are beautiful times we live in. They are also dangerous and bizarre times. The Prophecy of Purification is being fulfilled, and it is not a prophecy of doom or punishment. It is a prophecy of cleansing.

There is justice as well as balance in the natural order of the universe. We are all held accountable as I am held accountable for every word in this book.

I encourage each of you to test, to challenge, to investigate everything you read and learn. My students are instructed to assert themselves consistently (in gentle and reverent confrontation) regarding all information they receive through me. The medicine road is a path, a way of developing one's own personal medicine power. Be cautious not to give away your power to any teacher or to any belief system. Take what you learn with you; go alone in silence and in solitude and examine it. Ask for guidance from Earth Mother and Sky Father about a teacher or a group you are attracted to. Your mind may serve you or trick you. If you are attracted to, or repelled by, a teacher or certain knowledge, use the intuitive power of your soul to arrive at the Source and then to realize the reasons for the attraction or repulsion. Learn to use your own soul power. It will not trick you. My personal medicine tool of examination and effective investigation is the Medicine Wheel, the most powerful symbol in nature, the circle, the symbol of God.

Here is *Breath of the Invisible*. Although I am a Cheyenne-Arapahoe Indian, I speak in it only for myself and my warrior society. I am not an authority on the medicine. I am a servant of the medicine. I did my best in honesty, in humility. I did it for you. I did it for me. And I did it for those yet unborn. It is an account but also a dream. May it spark the growth of your medicine power and personal God communion.

Acknowledgments

We extend our special appreciation to the Wheelwright Museum of the American Indian in Santa Fe, New Mexico, and to the Heard Museum in Phoenix, Arizona, for their understanding and support of our artwork, even before we set foot in a gallery.

Special thanks to the Southwest Association of Indian Affairs (SWAIA) for creating the category of "Pipes and Pipebags" in their annual Indian Market at Santa Fe, to accommodate the judging of our artwork in Indian Market since 1978, and in their support of the ceremonial pipe as an art form.

Note: Native Indian terminology in this book is in either the Cheyenne or the Lakota (Sioux) language, which was adopted by the Indian Unity Movement in the early 1970s as the language of Indian unity during prayer and intertribal ceremony.

I

The Beginning, the Way, and The Tools

1
Bury My Heart With Medicine Rock

I returned home to western Montana in 1968 ready to "set all Indian tribes straight" with the acquired status of being the only family member to graduate from college. After a welcoming celebration by relatives, neighbors, and high school friends (many of us don't return), I found myself alone in a late night discussion with my grandmother. She asked me to tell her in one sentence the most valuable thing I had learned in college. I told her I had learned "what not to do." I also shared with her, gently, that it was my conclusion that our tribal rituals and ceremonies were harmful to us as a people striving to overcome poverty and hardship and "take our place in society." As an example of my meaning, I requested her to teach me the most effectively powerful ceremony she knew, one which would surely invoke a "spirit" to help me be successful in life. I promised to be attentive and obedient to her and to learn and to perform the ritual specifically as instructed. Although I approached her reverently, I was nonetheless arrogant. I told her that the ceremony would be no more than a fun thing to do, and I could prove this by doing it. She accepted

A college student climbed a mountain—
a warrior descended.

the challenge enthusiastically and agreed to teach me to "invoke the invisible" as an ally, as an intercessor.

I spent a summer in fasting and preparation. Then while fasting and with only a blanket, I went out alone to a special mountain far away in another state to experiment and test the ceremony. A natural stone platform extended out over the northern edge of the mountain. It took me a good part of the day to climb to the top.

As soon as I began the ceremony, feathers started to fall all around me, more and more of them. I kept looking up and all around. I never saw a bird, yet more and more feathers kept falling. Still no bird. I was not under the influence of any drug, herbs, or tea. I had fasted for one day.

The feathers were merely the beginning. I saw, felt, and heard several "manifestations." I was visited by more than one supernatural being of the invisible (yet visible) spiritual realm. I received a long-lasting "main vision," with glimpses of several visions yet to come after the completion of tasks and instructions. I discovered that such things as talons, feathers, paint, color, and ceremony were "tools," tools of self-realization as well as of communion with the spiritual realm. These specific instructions were guides to the use of attunement with "natural law," the order of the universe, whose organized components were spirit and matter, some frightening but all bringing enlightenment and wisdom.

It was at that time in that place—at the Valley of the Moon in the Cave of the Winds—that I was reunited with Earth Mother and Sky Father. I was now no longer an orphan but rather a relative to all that is. I became a morning star, a child of sun and moon.

I made a covenant with the pipe to follow the Red Road. I pledged my first sun dance as an offering of thanksgiving to the beauty I saw and the peace I felt in return for the knowledge I received. A spoiled college student climbed a mountain that day with a ceremony his grandmother taught him. A warrior descended.

For the next ten years I lived in a tipi and cabin, often alone, sometimes in a village with others, studying with Medicine People of different tribes. I hunted, tanned, carved stone, danced, prayed, and fasted. Today I am an artist, teacher, and ceremonial leader of the Redtail Hawk Society.

My grandmother, whose name is Medicine Rock, passed on soon after that summer when she taught me the ceremony. Later I lived in a village for awhile called Medicine Rock, where I took my first sweat ceremony with women. Medicine Rock showed me the Native American way which I have followed ever since.

2
The Red Road

Riverwoman is my best friend. She is also my business partner and the mother of our son Trinity. She is a Cherokee—a real one. My family has taken her in as a relative, and she loves the Cheyenne way. But she will always be a Cherokee.

We met twelve years ago in the woods on a river. She was fishing, and I crept up behind her Indian style. She is the best fisherman (fisherperson?) I ever met. She loves to eat catfish. She also loves cats. We call her the cat lady here at the ranch. The old woman down the road at the stone company says Riverwoman can tame any cat. Sometimes I have the tendency to fly high into the air, like the eagle, because I am a sun dancer. Riverwoman grounds me to Earth Mother.

River is, to my knowledge, the only Native American woman carving Plains ceremonial pipes. Her pipes are elegantly beautiful. She is best known for her bird pipes.

Riverwoman and I are being asked more and more by schools, churches, galleries, museums, and collectors of our artwork to come and speak on the meaning and inspiration of what we do, and of the role of our sacred pipe in our lives. Sometimes folks want to learn about our philosophy or culture or religion. But there is no philosophy or dogma or doctrine with us. We don't separate religion and culture. Our way of life is life itself, a living relationship and a living realization. We call it "the Red Road."

Red is the life color, the color of our most sacred carving stone, the "pipestone" known as catlinite. We call it "Shatunka," which is the Sioux word for red sacred stone. Red is the color of earth, of the rising and setting sun. It is the color of our skin, of our blood.

The Great Spirit is male and female. The male aspect of the Great Spirit is Sky Father, the female aspect is Earth Mother. All life is the child of Earth Mother and Sky Father. As sons and daughters of earth and sky, we are all related, not only to all races but also to plants, animals, and rocks. They are our relatives.

All life is subject to the "natural law" of the Great Spirit, which is order, balance, and harmony. Regardless of race or ideology, the sun sets in the west and rises in the east, on the Communist, the Catholic, the Anglo, and the Indian. The effects of the four seasons are experienced by the aspen, the eagle, the four-legged and the two-legged. All life is one with the same Source, even though there are differences and each is unique. This is one reason why we call the Great Spirit "the Great Mystery."

We are all held accountable to the same Source, which is truly a "Great Spirit." Those of us who strive for harmony and balance with one another and with the natural way of the Great Spirit are said to walk softly on the earth, to walk on the Red Road. One may be of any race or of almost any religion and walk the Red Road. The Road is a path, a way. Its full meaning is the way one acts, the methods one uses, and what directs one's doing. There is more to the Red

Road than spoken words or written words on paper. It is behavior, attitude, a way of living, a way of "doing" with reverence—of walking strong yet softly, so as not to harm or disturb other life. We are stewards, temporarily here to caretake the body we live in and the earth we live on, to fulfill our vision and individual destiny in harmony with one another and in balance with nature.

As we will see later, the sacred pipe is a tool and an altar with which we steer and center ourselves on the Red Road. It is also a way to commune with all our relatives—plant, animal, and mineral—and directly with the Great Spirit. For many Indians there is just the pipe, the earth we sit on, and the open sky. The spirit is everywhere. Simple living is less wasteful and more in harmony with nature, with Earth Mother. It permits a sharing of resources with all life. The basic necessities of life are the true luxuries. In speaking of our way of life, the Red Road, we speak of life itself: air, water, earth, sky, sun, moon, rock, plant, animal, the four winds, and the four seasons.

The universal thread of all life is breath. Without it life ceases. Animals, plants, and even rocks breathe. The winds breathe. We breathe into our pipes. In the pipe ceremony we share breath, we share smoke. The sacred smoke is the breath of life made visible, rising upward as a prayer to the Source of all breath, the Great Breath, the Great Spirit, which breathes individualized spirit as unique souls in unique creations, each unique yet all related. We are held accountable for the way we live, the manner in which we breathe. The tools given us by the Source of breath teach us how to breathe. The sacred pipe teaches us how to breathe. The Red Road shows us where to walk, softly, not treading on other life.

3
The Native American Prayer Pipe:
Breath Made Visible

Hear the words of Pte Ska Win (White Buffalo Maiden) as she appeared, walking from sky to earth, bringing the first of seven sacred gifts:

With visible breath I am walking. I walk and my voice is heard. I am walking with visible breath. I am bringing this sacred pipe, with it I walk to you. For you I am walking with this pipe . . . so that the breath may become visible.

To many people the story of White Buffalo Calf Maiden and the two young warriors who beheld her in the far North is categorized as "Indian myth" or "Native American legend." Yet the account of Moses on Sinai with the manifestation of the Lord Creator as burning bush, and the experience of Arjuna with Lord Krishna, these are accepted as "sacred scripture."

The weight and credibility of truth and wisdom in "sacred scripture" versus "myth" is obvious. Myths are generally classified as stories "created by" human beings in an attempt to find order in life, or to create solutions to the mystery of life's origin. Sacred scriptures, on the other hand, are accepted as knowledge from God, the Creator, the source of all existence, "communicated to" human beings by "revelation" in visions and dreams. No single civilization in history nor individual tribe of any continent has an exclusive monopoly on revealed visions from the Source and origin of all life. Moses was of a Semitic tribe, Arjuna an East Indian, and Crazy Horse an Oglala Sioux. They were all human beings, sons of Earth Mother and Sky Father.

Moses descended from Sinai with ten commandments. The warrior who respected Calf Maiden returned with the promise of seven gifts, the first being the sacred pipe, the tool which would teach the use and meaning of all seven gifts. With the smoking of the first sacred pipe, the ancient Native American elders of this continent discovered in spiritual communion that to share breath is to share life.

The sacred pipe is many things. To the casual observer, all prayer pipes are the proverbial "peace pipes." Although all pipes promote well-being, they have different functions. There are specific clan, society, personal, social, and council pipes. There are sun dance pipes, marriage pipes, and war pipes. There are pipe dances.

The prayer pipe is a ceremonial tool and a traveling altar. While leaning against a forked peg pressed and anchored in the earth, the pipe becomes a center of focus and concentration—an altar, similar to a mandala. When not smoked or used as such, the bowl and stem of a pipe are separated and wrapped individually but kept together. Usually a pipe is kept in a bundle or pipebag along with other things used in a pipe ceremony, such as tobacco and sweet grass.

The pipe is used in all Plains Native American ceremonies. It is the center of all we do; it is the "axis mundi" which forms a bridge between earth and sky, the visible and the invisible, the physical and the spiritual. The sacred pipe was brought to different tribes through different messengers, for the invisible spirit world is widely populated, as is the visible world. To the Blackfoot it was Thunder who brought the pipe, to the Arapahoe it was Duck. To many tribes it was White Buffalo Calf Maiden. It was the prophet Sweet Medicine who brought the arrow pipe bundle to the Cheyennes. And then there was Moses, and Arjuna with Lord Krishna.

The owner of a pipe bundle is sometimes known as a pipe holder or pipe carrier. Such a person must earn the privilege of owning a pipe bundle through instruction, preparation, tasks, and initiation. A pipe holder is respected as one whose priority in life is purity, and is thus requested by people to conduct ceremonies with the pipe. This is a sacred responsibility. A pipe holder is expected to observe a code of purity in feelings, words, and deeds.

The pipe and what it symbolizes is part of the Native American view of life. The Source and center of all existence is pure spirit existing in all created things simultaneously as Great Spirit. The absolute, unchanging, unmanifested invisible spirit is Sky Father; the manifested, ever-changing spirit becomes visible as nature in Earth Mother. The creator Source is male and female; all that exists is male or female. There are male and female plants, animals, rocks, and winds. There are male and female human beings.

All that exists is alive. All that exists is related, sharing a common Source, a common breath. Plants, animals, rocks, and people breathe. The winds breathe. The earth breathes. Earth Mother or Nature is the Creator's breath made visible. When there is concentration on, attention to, and recognition of this reality while one is smoking a prayer pipe, then a powerful transformation occurs. The smoke becomes sacred. The spirit of God in us all becomes visible as sacred smoke.

The experience is not accepted in common belief, but rather perceived in collective or individual spiritual communion with one another and with the divine Source itself. This is the beginning of the "making of medicine." The key is the acknowledgment, the connection, the experience of authentic self-realization, of authentic communication with the spirit world. Such phenomena are verified through individual experience.

The bowl of every pipe represents the female aspect of the Great Spirit; the stem represents the male aspect. The pipe bowl is Earth Mother; the pipe stem is Sky Father. The bowl is the earth, while the stem is all that grows upon the earth. The bowl is each person's head, and the stem is the spine.

The pipe bowl as Earth Mother aids in recalling to mind the acceptance of change in nature. Although we are in a sea of constant flux and change, there is warmth, order, and beauty in nature. When our lives are in harmony with other lives (our relatives), and if our will and behavior are in balance with the sustaining natural law (order) of the Creator, then we perceive and experience directly this warmth, order, and beauty of Earth Mother. If not, we experience confusion, chaos, disharmony and imbalance. Furthermore, we can bring other life with us in the whirlwinds of our confusion. This "other life" may be other people, the environment, or animals and plants.

There is medicine power in the four phases of the sun and moon and in each of the four seasons. Such is the rhythm of life. The day is regulated to the sun, the month regulated to the moon, and each year regulated to the seasons. The pipe ceremonies during the phases of the sun, of the moon, and of the four seasons assist us in accepting change, and sustain us during constant flux by anchoring us in the unchanging, in Source, in the Great Spirit. This is power.

The pipe stem as Sky Father is that which is unchanging and absolute in life. In the wheel of life and in the hub of motion, there is stillness in the center. The center is a compaction, a concentration of the power of all directions. There is a time appropriate for each of us individually, and sometimes collectively as clans, families, societies, or entire tribes, to withdraw from the wheel of motion in life and go to the center of the hub, to get centered, to become focused.

As there are earth and sky, the visible and the invisible, male and female, so there are two basic levels of native Indian experience—acceptance and transcendence. While Earth Mother teaches acceptance and nourishes us, Sky Father teaches transcendence and liberation, to gain release from harmful relationships, substances, desires. When a pipe is breathed into by exhaling, this calls attention to that which must be released or transcended. The puffs of smoke ascend from earth to sky. Inhaling while smoking a pipe brings smoke into the body and calls attention and realization to that which in life is accepted. The inhaling and exhaling of smoke is as the ebb and flow of life. The pipe is crucial as a tool in assisting an individual or a group to determine what is to be accepted and what is to be released.

This is the pipe. It is the bowl and it is the stem. Joined together, they yield the power of this realization.

Our ancient sages and contemporary elders assure us that the pipe and the sacred things associated with it are far from theoretical. The Great Spirit has specific principles manifested as natural order. The Creator continually and consistently reveals instructions: "If you do this, then this will happen." These instructions are timeless, revealed in nature and manifested as order and laws such as those governing motion, gravity, the phases of the sun and moon, and the seasons. We are not interested in abstractions. We take our pipes out as instructed to determine if they work. They do.

The sacred pipe is the center of the nation's hoop. Without it there is no life. This says it all and clarifies the sacred pipe's relationship to ceremony and life. We raise our children with the pipe, counsel alcoholics and drug addicts, resolve differences, heal the afflicted with it, celebrate life at sun dances, and, most important—it is the only tool we bring with us when we meet the Great Mystery, face to face, on a vision quest.

The sacred pipe is the "tool of tools," the most powerful and most cherished gift of all Native American Plains tribes. Today the use of the sacred pipe is being revived among many tribes, even those which traditionally did not use long-stem pipes. Furthermore, people of all races and ethnic backgrounds are journeying on vision quests, entering in sweat lodges, gathering at sun dances, and the pipe is always present.

Sacred things regarding the pipe are to be reflected upon and contemplated in the temple of silence on the altar of realization, not merely accepted and memorized in blind faith. In this way it can be understood why the first of the seven gifts from White Buffalo Calf Maiden was the sacred prayer pipe. For knowledge of the pipe is not enough. Just as training is useless without the honing of practice, so too knowledge of the sacred pipe without its use and practice as a "tool" will deem it a mere abstraction. To grasp fully the power and meaning of the sacred pipe using only the mind is to try to lasso the wind with a rope. Intellectual concepts cannot carry us to a destination but can only point the direction.

Ancient native sages and contemporary elders share with us in oral tradition that we two-leggeds, the human beings, were not created and then cast adrift in a sea of despair. Knowledge of the Creator and of the "Great Mystery" of life is hidden in everything created; the power of the sun is in every atom. Every person, animal, plant, or rock has a message or lesson, its medicine power. The more our perception is sharpened and our sensitivity purified, the less this presence of the divine in all things created seems secret or hidden. As direct communication with spirit increases, we respect creation more and worship only the source of creation.

The purpose of ceremony is to celebrate life and to sharpen our perception and "shanta-ista" (intuition). Some things are observed with the two eyes of the mind, and some things are known with the single eye of the soul, the shanta-ista. By observation of nature and vision-seeking, the native seeker learns about life from Source, which is more powerful than theology, doctrine, or dogma of mind. The mind is both a servant and a trickster. The sacred pipe is the central tool and guide to focus ceremony and symbol.

II

Invoking the Invisible through Ceremony

4

Symbol, Ceremony
and Source

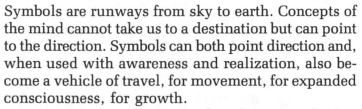

Symbols are runways from sky to earth. Concepts of the mind cannot take us to a destination but can point to the direction. Symbols can both point direction and, when used with awareness and realization, also become a vehicle of travel, for movement, for expanded consciousness, for growth.

We Native Americans translate the sun and other sacred powers into symbolic forms which have been revealed to us in visions and dreams. These symbols are worn or kept close by in painted designs or quilled or beaded items. We obtain power and wisdom through proximity, connection, and relationship to the symbols. These sacred objects are "antennas," to be cared for in a respectful manner. But only the Source of all power, the Great Spirit, is worshipped. We pray that the Great Spirit is everywhere and in all forms, and we worship it here through these symbolic forms.

I suggest that you go outside before continuing this book. Go alone, in silence. Sit comfortably under a tree. Breathe deeply seven times, and listen to the sound of your own breath for at least ten minutes. The

sound of breath will eventually calm you, without effort, without struggle. Don't try to slow your breathing. Just listen to it. As your inner restlessness is
calmed, reflect (don't analyze) upon the significance
of earth, sky, visible, invisible, form with mass, form
without mass. Shut off your mind and merely "visit"
with terms such as "realization," "awareness," "contemplation." What is the difference between knowledge and realization? How do the powers of
concentration and contemplation differ? If you can't
reconcile yourself to do this, there is no point in your
continuing to read on.

The ancient elders (and contemporary shamans) did
not possess these terms in their vocabulary, but they
practiced what they mean regularly. This was their
way to acquire enlightenment and wisdom and visions
of their higher self, their spirit guides, and of Source
itself. They also used symbols and ceremony to learn
to communicate and commune with the intelligent
consciousness of created things. They could communicate with animal, plant, rock, wind, water, or a spirit.
(Incidentally, when and if you ever decide to sit under
that tree again and breathe, visit awhile with the dis-
tinction between communication and communion.)

When a holy man or a healing woman sings out in
a ceremony, "All is alive, all are related," the implication is that all things created have a level of intelligence, be it a lordly elk or a pinch of cornmeal. For
example, a medicine person having knowledge and
use of rocks was trained by teachers and guided by
spirits to commune with rocks and is given direct information. He can communicate with the intelligent
consciousness of rocks, collectively and individually,
and exchange knowledge with them. Ceremony and
symbols are primary tools and vehicles to achieve this
exchange. When such an exchange occurs in harmony

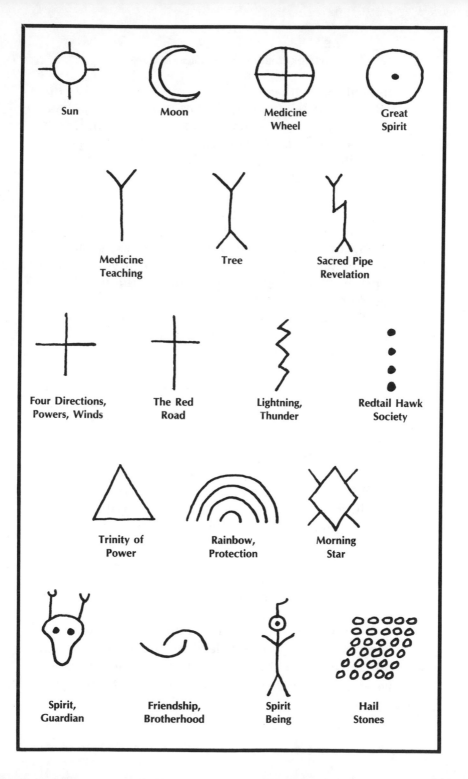

and balance with a rock, an intimate relationship develops. This relationship is part of medicine power,
as evidenced when a person summons the wind, calls
down an eagle, grows corn in an arid desert, heals the
sick with herbs, or raises consciousness with a specific
crystal. Each of us is capable of these things; this is
not an elitist phenomena.

The most difficult task in the preparation for communion with anything is the most crucial. It is not
letting one's mind, one's judgments, expectations,
and preconceptions interfere with intuitive soul perception. Our thoughts are located in the mind; our
life spirit manifested as soul is in every cell.

The sense consciousness of the finite body is a sensitive tool of perception, but it is limited to the five
senses bound to the physical, which grossly distract
us. The consciousness and subconsciousness of the
intelligent mind is a more powerful and less limited
tool, but it can trick us. The superconsciousness of
the intelligent soul is an unlimited tool. Combined
and balanced use of body, mind, and soul as tools of
perception (and as vehicles of movement and growth)
eventually yields unlimited expansion of consciousness and the capacity for direct union with the Great
Spirit. From such a union flows union with self and
with nature, with plants, animals, minerals.

Symbols and ceremony can be as blueprints for
these tools of perception and point us to the reality
behind them. They can also become vehicles of travel
to the destination of inner realization and outer awareness. Our knowledge, awareness, and realization increase through conscious and wilful communion with
our inner self, with other life forms in nature, and with
the spirit world. In this way our consciousness expands, preparing us to commune with Source, the

Great Spirit. All is connected. Each union leads to another. Knowledge without awareness and realization does not yield wisdom and is unbalanced. We shall see how ceremony uses symbols to lead us to the Source of all.

5

The Sacred Sweat

One of the seven sacred gifts and tools the Great Spirit sent to the two-legged humans through White Buffalo Calf Maiden was the ceremony of purification. The Creator in its infinite, omnipresent wisdom knew that mankind would deviate from the natural order and would also experience physical illness. The deviations in behavior are sometimes necessary for learning and growth; some illnesses are necessary for purification. So it is natural that a parallel system of purification be given to the people. A type of purification is performed to promote a pure self, cleansed and born anew, fit to be a vehicle of God. Healers and doctors, as direct channels through which the "great medicine" works, regularly purify themselves with a variety of tools such as the sacred sweat ceremony.

The rite of purification in the sweat lodge calls on all the powers of the universe: earth, water, fire, air, breath, and sky. We go in naked with only a loincloth and the pipe. Any jewelry or medicine objects to be purified are placed outside, usually on top of the lodge. The sacred pipe is used for prayer and offerings in the beginning. Then it is also removed from

The lodge of purification

the lodge and placed on a specially built dirt mound, with its stem facing East. The pipe thus becomes an altar for this ceremony.

A ritually built sweat lodge is erected of red willows for the sweat ceremony. As the willows are gathered from near a river, the gatherers sing a song to them, telling them how they will be used. A prayer is said, explaining that we come to gather willows as relatives, not as predators. A tobacco offering is left as a gift, for the gatherers go to nature to give and to receive, not merely to take what they want. The willows are gathered over a wide area and not all taken from the same place; this thinning strengthens the willow tribe instead of weakening it.

The site for the sweat lodge is cleared, and the center of the lodge is marked with a stake. This center represents the center of the universe. Prayers are said at the center, and the lodge area is smudged with cedar and sweet grass, as are those who are building the lodge. The lodge is made in the shape of a circle, with a willow frame over it, covered by hides or canvas. The door is to the East, for from this direction comes the light of new growth and wisdom. The whole lodge is a model of the universe.

A round hole is dug in the ground at the center of the sweat lodge, and with the dirt a sacred path (the "path of life") is made leading out of the lodge door to the East. At the end of the path is the fire hole where the rocks are heated. Each step is taken along this sacred path, with reverence and attention, for the lodge is to be built in a sacred manner with a good heart. We do all our sacred things in a circular and clockwise direction because this is the direction of the sun, which sends light, enlightenment, warmth, and growth down to earth. In order to prosper, we imitate the ways of earth and sky.

The fire outside the lodge used to heat the rocks (volcanic rocks are the best) is called the "fire of no end." To make this sacred fireplace, sticks are arranged in a certain way facing the four directions. After the fire is started (never using a lighter, only plain matches), it is alive, with an intelligence, wisdom, and purifying power. No garbage or paper is indiscriminately thrown into it.

The fire is never left alone. Usually the sweat lodge "tender" looks after it. This person does not take a sweat but remains outside to be of service. The lodge tender is said to be more blessed than those who take the sweat.

The rocks become white hot. Then they become red as molten lava. At this time they are ready to be taken down the path of life to the central pit inside the lodge. These hot rocks may be carried with a pitchfork, but some use a freshly cut "green" pole, forked at the end, as they don't like to use metal against the rocks or in the fire. I respect this.

While waiting for the rocks to heat, those preparing to take a sweat remain in the sweat lodge area, quietly reflecting and preparing. Now they enter into the lodge clockwise and sit in a circle. The pipe is handed in and passed around for each to smoke. Then it is handed out to the tender.

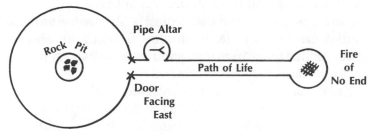

Sweat lodge, showing four circles of power

Each hot rock is carried down the path of life by the tender and individually guided to the central pit by the sweat ceremony leader, who usually sits in the West facing the eastern door. Each rock is named and commemorates a power or force in nature.

The approach to the sweat lodge varies among tribes. My personal vision and spiritual guidance has been that additions to traditional ceremonies and sacred ways can be made in a sacred manner, but we should never replace or compromise that which has gone before us and has been handed down.

The lodge door flap is shut and tucked in at the bottom. It is very dark inside. Only the glow of the red rocks in the central pit, the center of the universe, can be seen. It is hot. If you were there, you would already be sweating. You wouldn't be able to see the people next to you, but you could "feel" them there and hear them breathe.

The person next to you nudges you to get your attention, for you to receive the clay pot of drinking water. Each participant ceremoniously drinks a swallow of water, after which a drink is taken only if necessary. It is good to fast or eat lightly before sweating and to drink much juice or water beforehand.

Prayers of acknowledgment and thanksgiving are said for the rocks, fire, willow, earth, air, breath, and sky. Songs are sung; each participant who contributes a song of prayer does so voluntarily. Some remain quiet throughout the ceremony. Sometimes prayers are said for those in prisons and in hospitals. A prayer may be said for a sick relative.

Water or herbal teas are sprinkled on the rocks. The rocks begin to sing. You listen as the rocks speak. These ancient rocks have joined with fire and water in a trinity of power.

Now steam is formed. You learn quickly the difference in medicine power between the cool soothing water you drank and the steam you feel from the marriage of fire and water. The water as steam carries the Thunderbeings who usually come in storms but always bring goodness. As more water and teas are gradually sprinkled on the rocks, you inhale deeply the aroma of mint or spearmint and the sage you are sitting on. You rub your body with sage.

The sweat lodge tender outside signals to you that he is about to open the door flap temporarily. This is to remind you of the light outside, for in this ceremony the darkness represents your ignorance. The intensity of the sunlight outside is heightened by the darkness inside. Just as you are about to enjoy the soothing fresh air, the door flap is shut. You return to darkness. The sweat leader calls to mind the difference between darkness and the soothing comfort of a cleansed vision, a new sight.

Now much water and tea are sprinkled on the rocks. Body sweat comes fast, from head to toe. More water. The rocks are singing. More steam. Your sweat drips steadily now. Some inside are chanting. Some are breathing heavily. You all are sweating, breathing, and listening to the glowing rocks in darkness together.

The atmosphere inside the lodge is hot, damp, and dark, as in the womb of the Earth Mother. The lodge tender outside calls that he will open the door only if you need anything. More water and tea are sprinkled on the rocks. Now it is too hot to breathe through your nostrils. So you lie down, in humility, on the cool earth floor and breathe the "cooling breath" through your mouth.

Sometimes you hear yourself saying prayers or singing songs, and you do not know from where they come. A person calls out, "All my relatives," which means he wishes to go out and not return. Another calls to the tender, "I go out," which means he will go out but will return again. Each person remaining in the lodge helps guide those leaving the lodge, who often crawl down the path of life on all fours from weakness. We are weak, to be strengthened through purification in this sacred rite. As people leave, the door flap is open and shut quickly so as not to lose heat and steam.

More water and tea are sprinkled on the rocks. Now the bottom of the lodge seems as hot as the top. You find yourself trying to forget your body. In doing so you are forced inward, deeply, and then outward, beyond. Your whole body feels like one big open sweat pore. You feel very weak, as though you are about to pass out. Then suddenly you feel a subtle surge of strength that seems independent of the body. Your breathing deepens and slows down. You feel your lungs filling all the way to the top of your chest beneath your neck, instead of only to your abdomen as before.

The sweat leader asks you if you wish a drink of water. As you drink, you feel the cold water explode into your head, as if the inside of your mouth were absorbing the life power of water. It is. You hold the water in your mouth awhile before swallowing; you feel it, savor it. As you swallow, each part of your body is heightened in sensitivity, and you feel the water as it progresses from throat to chest to belly and beyond. You experience the power of water. You experience firsthand the difference in spirit and power between cool flowing liquid water and steam, water transformed by fire and rock into the power of thunder.

You want another drink, but your attention is drawn to an inner voice, counseling you about some problems with habits you are having. After awhile you find yourself struggling to pay more attention to this inner voice. You have been distracted from the experience by thinking, by analyzing, by asking who or what is this voice: "Is it me or is it God?" Instead of flowing and experiencing the voice, you struggle to classify and categorize it in concepts of logic and reason. At that point the voice ceases.

Suddenly there is a glow opposite you. You blink your eyes to clear away the river of sweat. The glow brightens. The sharp image of an old man slowly develops in front of you across the rock pit, as if formed out of white smoke. You sit up, startled. The old man has white braids wrapped with crystals of ice. He opens his eyes and looks at you; his eyes are blue opals.

Someone calls out, "All my relatives!" The door flap is swung open, sunlight enters, and the person next to you begins to crawl out of the lodge. The lodge tender asks if anyone else wants to go. Spontaneously you call out, "All my relatives!" You think to yourself as you crawl out, "I'm not ready for all this." Once outside you regret leaving.

You can hardly stand up. Your body is steaming. The lodge tender helps you to the creek. The blue sky is crisp, the green trees so fresh. You feel cleansed inside and out. You submerge yourself slowly in the cold creek and experience yet another facet of the crystal power of water. It is so cold that it makes you see stars and flashes of light. As you climb out of the creek, a friend hands you a blanket. He tells you that you were in the lodge for hours. It seemed less than an hour.

You stand tall, lighter; you have left behind pounds of ignorance and impurity. You feel as a child newly born. You recall the teaching of Jesus Christ's counsel: "You must be born again of water and of spirit." You also think about what the alchemists really meant by the transformation of lead into gold. You sit around the "fire of no end" with the others who had left the lodge before you. It is quiet. No one is speaking. Each is either staring into the fire or looking up at the sky. Everyone is smiling. You feel a smile on your face so large it is as from ear to ear. Everyone looks fresh, clean, and peaceful.

You look back at the sweat lodge as the lodge tender opens the door flap to let the last person out. As he crawls out, you think you see the old man glowing inside the lodge. But he is gone. You look harder, more intently, but you can't see him. He is gone.

There will be another day, another sweat. The lodge tender raises his arms to sky and sings, "The circle is complete." The sweat ceremony leader replies, "May we all see more clearly so that we may increase

in a sacred manner.'' The sweat lodge purification ceremony is over.

A crow flies overheard from the East to the West.
Several blue jays flutter in the elms next to the sweat
lodge. A swarm of bees dances around the wild mountain flowers.

6
The Vision Quest

I am still.
I listen and see the silence.
I listen and embrace the silence.
I enter into the great silence.
Though hidden, Grandfather dwells in all.

A discussion of the Native American Indian vision quest invites comparisons with the samadhi of the yogi, the satori of the Zen Buddhist, and the ecstacy of the Christian mystic. There are universal characteristics of illumination common to all three of these. The basic aim of each is to enter into the inner silence in order to embrace the outer silence.

The purposes of the vision quest are to discover one's self—one's destiny, one's relation to earth—and to discover one's medicine power, and also to contact God directly. Commonly, we view God as a distant creator eager to administer justice on us for breaking a law or restriction. Preoccupied with guilt, we seek forgiveness, or forget about the whole situation by burying ourselves in excessive pleasure and indulgence. Such a situation is present in every culture, among all peoples—in some more than in others. The vision quest achieves liberation from the

33

concept of a legalistic Lord and opens us to a living relationship with an indwelling spirit, to a personal relationship with an omnipresent Great Spirit.

In addition to being alienated from God, we generally experience daily alienation from one another, and we do not know ourselves. We are spiritually sad at our alienation and our separation from knowing who we are, from our destiny, from our medicine power, and from the nature of our relationship with other forms of life. We are also alienated from nature. We don't view ourselves as at home in the wilderness, on earth as Mother, beneath sky as Father. Rather, we are frightened of nature and feel "exposed" to the elements. We feel it is ourselves against nature and try to gain dominion over it in order to survive the natural forces assaulting us. Native Indian consciousness and spirituality reconcile this alienation and eliminate the fear, especially through the vision quest.

The quest begins with the discovery of self, but its purpose is communion directly with Father-Mother God, either in manifested aspects and activities or with absolute non-manifestation. Our role in this communion is to discover our identity and destiny so that we can support the order of the universe in coexistence with creation. Through the quest, we are to discover our individual medicine and power. Our tools are all creation, which is the body of the Great Spirit, and every act is one of worship. The final stage is our awareness of identity with God and our interconnectedness with creation.

The reward of the vision quest is the unending joy of deliverance and liberation from suffering through our communion of self with Source, the ultimate, unchanging Great Spirit. The discovery of our individual "medicine" gives us an anchor in the world of instability and constant change. As warriors, our vision

and medicine power enable us to be strengthened by
our adversaries, not intimidated by them. The enemy
may be an external threat or an internal shadow, such
as a habit, thought, or feeling. Two of the verifications
of authentic vision and God communion are the experiences of joy and bliss. Unlike pleasure and happiness, they are perennial and will not fade. One can
be temporarily dissatisfied or unhappy, but the under-
lying joy and peace remain unchanging, anchored in
the absolute reality of Spirit. Those in touch with their
medicine power as a result of vision may experience
pain, but they never suffer. Their untouchable inner
realization has revealed to them that pain is natural
and that it is always temporary. Suffering is unnatural.
There is nothing that was created to suffer. Suffering
is unending. The victory of the vision is power and
peace in spite of negative circumstances, not in the
absence of them.

Many students and seekers come to me requesting
to learn about power, the pipe, feathers, or the peyote.
I usually settle them down from their questions and
begin their preparation for a vision quest. Even young
children on the Red Road, after learning the Medicine
Wheel, prepare for a vision quest.

One on a vision quest goes out alone, naked, exposed to nature's elements, carrying only a pipe and
a blanket. The length of time spent varies with each
individual's pledge, usually one to four days of fasting and praying. The quest begins with crying out and
lamenting for a vision because we seek reconciliation
from the alienation we feel from nature, God, and ourselves.

Long before going out, the seeker has been preparing, and the preparation is as important as the quest
itself. Specific practices involve training and instruction for body, mind, emotions, and spirit, so that the

preparation is total and complete. The vision seeker has many tasks to perform, for training without practice is as ineffective as a dull blade, which tears instead of cutting.

Training of the emotions involves learning to deal with fear. A seeker not emotionally prepared for a possible visual encounter with a spirit being may become weakened psychologically instead of heightened or strengthened. In all preparations for any instruction, any ceremony, or the vision quest, we are guided by the admonition, "Be attentive. Do not be afraid." Sometimes this is all we are told. This counsel must be understood. It does not mean that we should fear nothing or be macho or cocky. We all experience fear, but a warrior is not intimidated by fear. To face fear head on is to be a warrior. If we won't face fear, then we must be walking with it. To see fear in a detached manner is not to be connected to it. To view fear is different from becoming afraid. Most fear is created by the individual within himself. When a fear arises, from external or internal reasons, a warrior beholds it and is attentive in order to determine its source and movement: "This fear is here. OK, where did it come from? What's it going to do now? Where is it going? Is it from inside myself? Is it from an external threat or harm?" This is how one prepares emotionally.

Preparation involves different concepts, rituals, and spiritual exercises for different people with different modes of awareness, levels of consciousness, and types of emotional temperament. It is an advantage to have an instructor as a personal guide, preferably a shaman or medicine person. Nevertheless, I advise and encourage you, whatever your age, race, awareness level, or temperament, to go in solitude and merely sit in silence, to relax, to observe nature, and when comfortable, to close your eyes from the outside world and enter into your "inside world." After awhile, sit still and observe the natural world around you.

The common denominator in preparations for all people for the vision quest is purification of body and mind. The purification involves specific observances and abstinences regarding diet, behavior, and prayer. Purifying the body and mind strengthens the spirit. As we purify ourselves, we concentrate our power. The power is already there; we go on a vision quest to realize it and gain communion and assurance from God. Purification also focuses our inner center and sensitizes us for new perceptions.

This total purification occurs in the sweat lodge through the ceremony and the rite of purification. Some students seem "let down" when they experience a visionary revelation in the sweat lodge in preparation before their vision quest. They feel their vision alone on the hill will be short-changed. But this is linear, sequential thinking, not circular thinking. The way of Spirit is not a linear succession of events but an unending circle of interconnectedness.

Linear thinking uses only the intellect of the mind. Circular thinking uses the mind guided by intuition. A linear attitude is concerned with the end product only and not with process. It is overshadowed by preconceptions and expectations. It measures time in a straight-line (linear) schedule instead of a circular flow. A linear attitude is concerned with expectations of "I want." It is burdened with preconditions such as "I'll do this to get that," instead of valuing the process of doing as well as the getting. A circular attitude is one of nonattachment to the getting; it enjoys the doing and is not preoccupied with deadlines. Rather, it flows with "it will happen when it's supposed to happen." Linear thinking is a barrier in understanding medicine teachings.

Those with the highest expectations and preconceptions will be tested most. Expect nothing, receive all. Expect everything, receive nothing but the lesson of expectations. (In actuality, we test ourselves. But I won't explain that. You reflect on it.)

A basic aim of mental purification for the vision quest is to gain control of bodily indulgences, which also sharpens the spirit, and to silence the thinking mind so that it shifts its awareness from the rational to the intuitive mode of consciousness. We learn to develop the "shanta ista," the third eye of seeing beyond the two eyes of knowing. We sharpen the blade of our senses to behold carefully the manifestation of God in changing nature and commune with God in nature. We commune with God internally through introspection of God's nature in us.

The mind is but a fractional part of total being. It can trick us or serve us. Our total being involves body, mind, heart, and spirit. The logic and reason of the abstract thoughts of our conscious mind are strong tools, yet they are limited and often distracting. The intuitive wisdom of our superconscious shanta ista is unlimited and provides direct insight into the true nature of things as created by Source. This insight is beyond the realm of the mind. When we see with a unified total being, we are beyond the intellectual framework of concepts. We venture beyond the model. We cease studying the blueprint and enter into the Grand Architect's natural world. There is a time and a necessity for a briefing with the blueprint. But then arrives a point in time when the blueprint is set aside. This is the time to go out alone, naked, exposed, to face the Great Mystery and embrace the Great Silence.

Rational knowledge is important and not to be dismissed. It is essential in dealing with the objects and events of our daily life. It belongs to the intellect which measures and compares. Its movement is linear, as indicated by its prime mode of expression—language and analysis. As we grow comfortable using this rational tool, we establish a dependency on it and its priority. Eventually we become dominated by mind, held in bondage to measuring and categorizing, leading to a fragmented view of the natural world. The relationship and interconnectedness of all things is then merely speculated on instead of experienced. Centeredness and connectedness are replaced by alienation. Sons and daughters of Earth Mother and Sky Father are no longer fulfilled by the natural world. Such a condition is out of balance with life in nature. We then hear a call from the sweat lodge, "All my relatives." The mind says, "Wait, how can that be? Is this rock my cousin? Is that dog my brother? It doesn't fit into any compartments of my rational mind. If it doesn't fit, it can't be!"

Many seekers are afraid to leave the comfortable and assuring stronghold of the familiar avenues of their rational minds. Yet this is the most crucial part of a vision quest preparation and also the most difficult. Many feel stupid when requested to hug a tree or talk to a rock. The task of guiding students to practice spiritual exercises which will prevent thinking from interfering with experiencing is the most difficult task I've encountered in working with students. Some get the impression that I am requesting blind acceptance, but this is not the same as humble surrender. On the Red Road we are requested to "face" certain tasks with "eyes open," with an aura of self-realization, not blind dogma.

The releasing and silencing of the rational mind is

enhanced by the actual experience of the vision quest itself. This is achieved in preparation for the quest by emptying and relaxing the mind and focusing attention on just one thing. We become restless due to the constant changes and sensory bombardments in our daily lives. Everyone is restless; only the degree of restlessness varies among us. The lake of our inner total consciousness is rippled by the winds of survival and struggle. We cannot control the struggle. We can, however, minimize or maximize our degree of restlessness, not in a repressed constrained manner, but as the tail of the hawk "steers" it in flight. The tail does not control the wind; it steers and works in harmony with wing and body and contributes to a smooth, safe flight.

We learn to empty, relax, and concentrate the mind by "listening" to our own breath. By sitting still in silence and listening to the inhaling (Earth Mother) and exhaling (Sky Father), we calm the restlessness within us. Our lake of consciousness becomes placid as a mirror and reflects clearly, accurately, and vividly the images near it, so that they are not distorted by ripples of restlessness. The more deeply and completely we breathe, the deeper we delve in consciousness. As we go deeper, consciousness expands. What we thought was a lake becomes an ocean.

As our consciousness expands, it rises to higher levels. We have risen to the sky. Now we journey out of and beyond ourselves. We discover the unity between the Within and the Beyond. Not that we are thinking about it—we are seeing it; we are experiencing it. Breath reveals itself as the living link between body, mind, and spirit. We share breath with creation and with its Source. The inner experience and outer communion become visible to us. This is the way we prepare to face the Great Mystery in the Great Silence.

After instruction and purification, the vision seeker pledges to go out from one to four days and nights, to a special place on Earth Mother. Some places are power vortexes where spirits are known to dwell— mountain tops, cliffs, some caves, washes (arroyos), or a vision pit dug for the purpose. A person may be guided as to where to go (or for how long) in a dream, or instructed by his or her teacher or helper. But wherever he goes, he goes alone, carrying only a pipe and a blanket. A seeker who pledges to go out for one day usually goes at sunset and returns at sunset of the following day. His instructor or helper escorts him to the place where he will do his vision quest. After smoking the pipe with him, the helper counsels and advises him regarding his vision and then leaves.

The seeker then goes to the spot for the quest. He draws a circle on the earth around himself noting the four directions and center of this circle. The symbol of God is the circle, and the movement of God is in all directions. The directions vary and commemorate the seasons and the phases of sun and moon. But the center of the circle, the eye of the Creator, is motionless and unchanging. That which changes is set in motion and initiated from that which is changeless. How is this? Such is the Great Mystery, to be continually reflected upon, from which comes enlightenment and wisdom. Enlightenment is knowledge of the self; wisdom is knowledge of the world.

Next the vision seeker makes an offering to the Great Spirit with a pipe or tobacco or cornmeal. A prayer is offered, telling the "Great Silence" and its four powers who he is and what he seeks, invoking their guidance and help. For days and nights the seeker smokes, performing the ceremony of the making of sacred smoke in a circle. He moves to each of the four directions but spends most of the time in the center. He sleeps in the center, remaining inside the circle always.

All that has been said about the pipe—the meaning of the stem and bowl, the act of making breath visible, of sharing breath with all creation and with God—happens in this vision circle. When not smoked, the pipe is held in hand or set in the circle as an altar and contemplated. In the use of the pipe, all elements are joined in communion: the stone bowl, wooden stem, fire, air, and breath. The plant, animal, and mineral kingdoms are represented. This is one of the many ways the sacred prayer pipe is used as both a ceremonial object of spiritual communion and a tool of self-realization.

If you go on a vision quest, you will find yourself alone, between earth and sky, with a pipe and a blanket in your circle, with no food but perhaps some water. Your mind is empty. Your body is purified and sensitized. Your spirit has been sharpened by tasks and preparations for months.

Your place is here. Your time is now. Will you be shaken or embraced by the powers of God—Father, Mother, Source, Grandfather? Will a divine communication come in direct revelation from God or through a spirit messenger? Will the spirit messenger be a spirit power or come through an animal or plant or a rock?

You stop questioning and empty your mind. Then you take some deep breaths. After counting seven deep breaths, you relax and listen to your breath at its own pace. As you inhale, you mentally chant "Earth," and you chant "Sky" as you exhale. You stand up and raise your pipe to the sky and then lower it to earth. Closing your eyes, you lie down at the center of the circle. It is your circle of life, your center. Regardless of the grief and turmoil in the world, you are at your center. You experience a peace not found in the world, but only in the person who walks the path in the world. Lying there, you know you have the power to journey deep within yourself or to journey out and observe nature or to journey beyond both. You know that, though seemingly hidden, the Great Spirit dwells in all. You wonder again if your vision will take the form of inner perception, sound, light, symbol, joy, love, wisdom, color, a person, rock, or plant. Will you receive a name or a song or perhaps a special prayer, to be used only between you and God?

You listen to breath again. As you breathe, your whole body pulsates. Your mind is pulsating. The ground beneath you is pulsating. The pulsations are slow, rhythmic, and very strong. Then a woman's voice begins to sing: "Have good will to all true religions, love them in your heart—but be loyal to the path Father Sky will show you. Stick to what you receive." You jerk your head up and look around. No one is there. You smile and close your eyes again. Then you think of the words of some sacred scriptures you have read. Although when you read them, you made no attempt to memorize, they come forth:

> They shall call on my name, and I will hear.
> You will pray and I will answer.
> You will call, the Lord will answer, "Here I am."
> The Bible

> He who sees me in everything and everything in me, is never separated from me, nor I from him.
> The Bhagavad-Gita

A warm feeling of well-being surges within you—arms, legs, all over. You realize that to see the relationship of all creation intellectually is exciting, but to experience the interconnectedness of all life is more real. It is to feel compassion for all beings, and also to feel the collective compassion of all beings toward you.

You feel a chill. You open your eyes and see the sun going down. You move to the western point of your circle and offer your pipe and sacred smoke to the setting sun. Then you move back to the center of your circle, lie down, and wrap yourself in your blanket. You place your pipe on the ground, at arm's length, with its stem pointing East, ready to greet the rising sun of the forthcoming day. Flocks of blue jays hustle to a grove of cedars to bed down for the night. Nighthawks begin to nosedive and soar in all directions. You behold. You are attentive.

After awhile you feel like there is sawdust in your eyes and you decide to sleep. It has been a full day. You have fasted and sweat, both in prayer and in ceremony, both in celebration and in preparation. Tomorrow you will greet the rising sun and the morning star. Tomorrow you will be out, all day, alone, yet not alone, from sunrise till sunset. You will stay in your circle out on this hill in this hidden valley.

You pray for guidance to come in your dreams. You pledge in prayer to do a vision quest once a year for the rest of your life. You know that the vision quest is the beginning of a search that must last all your life, that visions are to be renewed and kept pure, not diluted by wishful thinking or by daily living. You want the rest of your life to be a vision quest, a quest of visions.

As you close your eyes ready to sleep, the nighthawks dive down closer to you. You call out, "A-ho brothers." Tonight is a good night to sleep and to dream. Tomorrow is a new day, a new dawn, a new light, with new realizations. Tomorrow will be a good day to die, a good day to live. Tomorrow will be a good day for a vision quest, a good day to breathe, to share breath with earth and sky and all in between.

7

Medicine Wheel I:

The Circle, the Spirits, and the Totem

The Circle

Of all existing symbols, the most universally occurring in nature is the circle. It is the approximate shape of Earth Mother, Grandmother Moon, Father Sun, and other planets. It is essentially the shape of planetary orbits and the path of smoke rising from fire. It is the shape of the nests of the winged ones, the hunting patterns and territorial markings of animals, and the growth patterns in trees, flowers, and rocks. Biochemical reactions that comprise the physiology of body, as well as the thought processes of mind, are cyclic. Psychological behavior patterns are cyclic. The shape of the eye and the pupil are round. The shapes and orbits of atoms and molecules are circular, as are eggs and the seeds of life. The entrance to the womb and all open orifices to the body are circular.

The natural order of collective life in nature is symmetry, harmony, and balance, with a circular movement of ebb and flow. The circle has neither beginning nor end, for the beginning is the end and the end is the beginning. Some physicists claim that every existing symbol can be superimposed on a circle. Some mathematicians boast the circle to be the most perfect symbol. Many architects claim the circle to be the most structurally sound arrangement.

It is the symbol of the circle which yielded the wheel, an application of symbol that revolutionized human life. The wheel is the most invaluable human invention, providing the basis of movement in cars, trains, wagons, and bicycles. The circular wheel is

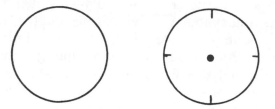

at the basis of machinery in pulleys and ball bearings. The path of reduced resistance for movement is the wheel: the minimizing of strength against weight and gravity is the circular pulley.

It is not surprising then when native elders and sages tell us that their revelations and visions revealed the Creator Source, God the Great Spirit, as a circle, a circle of white light. The circle is the universal sum of all symbols, as white is the totality of all color. The most powerful and most universally occurring symbol in nature, the circle, is the omnipresence of the Great Spirit existing in everything created, everywhere, at all times. It is Source manifested as symbol.

The symbol for both life and the Great Spirit is the circle. It is the most powerful protective and healing symbol, on many levels and in many ways. The shape of a warrior's shield is circular, a doctor's healing motion of massage on a patient's body is often circular. Often the healing ceremony itself occurs within a circle drawn around a patient. Native lodges and drums are circular. The sound of the drum is the rhythm and pulsation of life. Without the circle there is no life. Our forefathers perceived that if the circle of the nation's hoop was broken, then the buffalo would disappear, the land would be taken, and warriors would lose power.

The circle as the symbol of God has a center, the eye of God, and four major directions and movements, each emanating from and returning to the center. The three aspects of the Creator—trinity—together with its four major movements—the seasons and the four directions—comprise the number seven. Our individual souls pass through seven circles of energy along the cerebro-spinal axis, corresponding to the seven days of creation, the seven colors of the rainbow, and the seven sacred rites of the Oglala Sioux.

There are ''seven sisters'' or stars of the Pleiades constellation. These seven stars in conjunction with the spring and autumn equinoxes were used in ancient times by Plains tribes for medicine in planting and harvesting. According to information handed down, the seven sisters were placed in the heavens as seven stars, but one of them hid and only six are visible. This is testimony and reminder that, although the Great Spirit reveals and manifests itself for teaching, communication, and communion, it will always remain ''the Great Mystery,'' to be continually and endlessly contemplated in this life.

Although the Great Spirit, Source, and All-Father has innumerable aspects and manifestations, it revealed itself to native ancients on the American continent as a circle—the circle of life, the hoop of the people—of white light, whose numbers are three, four, and collectively seven. Color, symbol, and number are to be intuitively contemplated. They provide big medicine for healing and protection as well as great power for growth and expanding consciousness among Northern Plains tribes.

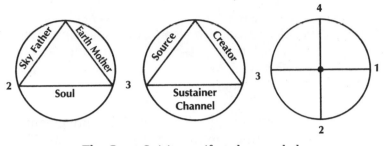

The Great Spirit manifested as symbol,
number, and color (white light)

As stated previously, attempts to analyze such phenomena intellectually are confusing and can reveal
only the finger pointing to the moon. There is a time
for mind and thinking and a time for no-mind and not
thinking.

The Circle as Medicine Wheel

The medicine circle has been used by native people for centuries. They knew about its power, protection and wisdom and used it often. The medicine
wheel is as powerful and effective today as it has been
for centuries.

The symbol of the circle can be ceremoniously constructed, with its center and four directions marked.
This will become a Medicine Wheel if it is used properly. It becomes a vehicle for determining the balanced
direction of the growth of consciousness. Or it can
show the movement of one's realization and awareness or be an anchor and focal point for centering self.
Or spiritual communion with the supernatural invisible world can come through the Medicine Wheel. The
Medicine Wheel can be many things: tool, guide, anchor, symbol, vehicle, map, or as circle of protection
for sacred ceremonies.

The Medicine Wheel is basically simple; it is a symbol (circle) with a single center and four directions.
When not kept simple, it ceases to be what it is and

loses power. Constructing a Medicine Wheel is a ceremony, a celebration, a testimony. It also acknowledges the divine Creator, its involvement and flow in every direction, and its existence as the center and Source of all things created.

Spirits of the Medicine Wheel

Of all the spirits populating the invisible world, there are four most friendly to man. They are said to be Mondaman (friends of human beings). They are the servants of Maheo (God), messengers to human beings, and act as guardian angels for each of the four cardinal points of the universe. When a Medicine Wheel is properly set up, these spirits are summoned. Although not all spirits come when summoned, these Mondaman spirits always come. Whether or not each reveals itself depends on the seeker and on God. Each of these four spirits is a spirit keeper of one of the four directions (and winds) of the circle of life, the Medicine Wheel. They are sacred persons, the great Maheyuno who guard creation. Sometimes they reveal themselves in visions as beings on horseback, the color of each horse corresponding to the color of its direction. My brother, White Eagle, saw the white spirit rider of the North while fasting and praying at Medicine Rock.

In Cheyenne sacred art, these spirit keepers are pictured as beings with forked horns. Each Maheyuno's body is painted the color associated with the direction it guards and keeps. Although the four sacred spirit keepers are friendly, the spirit keeper of the West often tests you with thunder and lightning. Some spirits, such as Mescalito or the Thunderbird, are not always friendly. All spirits teach and bring good, but some are terrifying and test as well as teach. Some spirits will embrace you; others will shake you. The four spirit keepers will share their wisdom concerning the working of things. However, these Maheyuno must be respected. A seeker must show veneration and respect in a sacred manner, usually through prayer and fasting. Then one or all of the Maheyuno will appear and be revealed. Each will impart a share of its wisdom and power and offer protection. The spirit keepers are mentioned by name in prayer. The pipe is offered, and the seeker requests each Maheyuno to draw near, to smoke with him, to share breath, and to hear his request. In past days, Cheyennes used to come out of their tipis at dawn, with their arms extended toward the East. They were asking the spirit keeper of the East to give them life for the day ahead.

Under the Great Spirit Maheo, the spirit keeper of the East is the sacred person who originates life and light, corresponding to the new life of spring and the new light of the sunrise. I still extend my arms to the East regularly at sunrise. Often this is the way I begin my day creating artwork in my studio. My studio faces East and the southern tip of the Rocky Mountains.

We Cheyennes always invite the four sacred persons, Maheo, and Earth Mother (Esceheman) to smoke with us, to share breath. We ask Earth Mother to make water flow so that we may drink, to keep the ground firm that we may walk upon it, to allow plants and herbs to be used in healing ceremonies, and to cause the grass to flourish for food for animals. These are some of our prayers used in the wheel, using it as a means to commune with earth and sky.

The universe is filled with other spirits, collectively known as Maiyun, who may assume the forms of animals, birds, natural forces, or the form of a young woman. Sun is among the greatest of these powers; thunder is among the strongest.

Ghosts, or Mistai, are rarely seen but are sometimes felt or heard. They are spirits derived from the dead, not the ghosts of specific people. Mistai is the same Cheyenne word used for owl. I will speak more about the owl later. The Mistai linger near earth, restlessly somewhere between life and death. But most souls shake free of their earthly bodies in death and travel along the Milky Way to Se'han, a formless (or form without mass) non-dimensional, immeasurable continuation of spirit. Little is known about Se'han, and this is as it should be, for we are more concerned with life on earth beneath the sky. But we do know that there is a life of the soul before the womb, in the womb, after the womb, and beyond death. Perhaps life beyond death is as life before the womb. We also know that Se'han is a pleasant existence near or in Maheo. Although there is no punishment in Se'han, there is perfect justice and mercy and order. Therefore, perhaps some souls remain in Se'han, while others must return to the womb. A holy man once mentioned that an infant cries at birth because its soul does not want to return from Se'han. But we are on earth, so let us go to the Medicine Wheel.

The Medicine Wheel provides a relationship with Maheo and the four Maheyuno in the symbol of the circle, using color and direction. This relationship is a partnership. It is not enough to acknowledge these powers and forces; a seeker learns how to get them to respond. Coming into harmony means entering into a sacred partnership, and each must do his share. It is a working relationship instead of blind faith and waiting for things to come. The Medicine Wheel used as a tool is essential in discovering one's path and then in maintaining it on the Red Road. Visions are renewed on a continuing basis. Most native religions are based on personal power, not to be given away or handed over to an organization or institution. The Medicine Wheel exalts the personal power of Maheo (the life force) flowing through all creation. Medicine is something you caretake and work with regularly.

To understand truly the significance of the Medicine Wheel, it will help to sit under a tree from time to time, reflecting and breathing, as I taught you before. Much has been shared to reflect about. Why do I suggest a tree? I encourage you to question all I share with you, in the silence of contemplation, on the altar of reverence. Reverence does not imply acceptance. It is a matter of gentle assertion, of respectful investigation using the total perception of body, mind, and soul.

Regarding the tree, a most respected pipe instructor, Robert Swiftotter, a Kiowa pipeholder, told a gathering atop a mountain in 1972 that "to be Indian was to hug a tree." That was all he said. Most folks there thought he was being arrogant and sarcastic. They were expecting an esoterical, mystical discourse from him. Trees, I have since learned, are transitors of energy between earth and sky. Currently, I am learning the language of trees from Seneca. Trees are "grounded" and are very still. Entering into a sacred relationship with a tree clears perspective and calms restlessness. As the lake of our inner consciousness is calmed, it reflects clearly, as a mirror, that which we are contemplating. The surface of a restless rippling lake reflects many moons, yet there is but one moon. The placid surface of a calm lake reflects one moon, clearly, distinctly. Hug the tree before, and after, you sit beneath it to listen, to breathe, and to reflect.

The Cardinal Points

The center of the Medicine Wheel is motionless, the eye of God. We Cheyennes call this center "the blue sky," where the Creator resides, where all direction, medicine, power, quality, and perspectives are compacted and concentrated, from which existence flows, to which existence returns.

The four directions are marked on the wheel, and there is a spirit keeper to caretake each. Each of the directions has its specific color, animal, plant, mineral, and the spirit keepers are connected with these. There are many other things connected with the directions and their spirits:

quality	season
power	time of life
direction, movement	phase of existence
wind	perspective
time of day (phase of sun)	element medicine
time of month (phase of moon)	

All of these have a position on the wheel that corresponds to the direction they are connected with; one thing leads to another. All ceremonial movement is in relation to the motionless center. Such is the will of Maheo, the Great Spirit.

The colors, animals, plants, and minerals of the four
cardinal points on the Medicine Wheel may vary from
tribe to tribe. Some tribes extend the wheel to twelve
points, as each spirit guide caretakes three moons
(months) with twelve corresponding clans for the
twelve months of the year. This is invaluable in providing a type of "earth astrology" and bringing folks
closer to earth and grounding them. So many folks
are concerned with the planets and stars "out in
space" instead of discovering their own place on
earth. Although I am primarily concerned with the
center and the four major directions, I applaud this
twelve-point extension of the wheel. It draws attention to the versatility and graceful flow of nature. The
south wind, for example, enters into combination with
the west wind, providing a southwest wind.

The circumference of the Medicine Wheel represents one's self discipline and one's private space or
inner territory in life. To be out of the circle of life
is to be out of harmony with life and out of balance
with one's self, one's center. Such a condition is alienation, from which other ills arise. The intelligent consciousness of the Creator, Maheo, is in color, wind,
plants, animals, rocks, and in you. It is the Spirit of
the Creator existing in all, collectively called the Great
Spirit.

Totems

Each of us enters the wheel of life at a specific point
at our birth. This is our beginning place on the wheel.
Our very beginning, our birth, gives us certain powers and responsibilities. Before we ever go on a vision
quest or perform any tasks of preparation, a gift of
power is bestowed upon us by God, in grace, just by
virtue of our existence. We were created by Maheo
and have power, purpose, and responsibility.

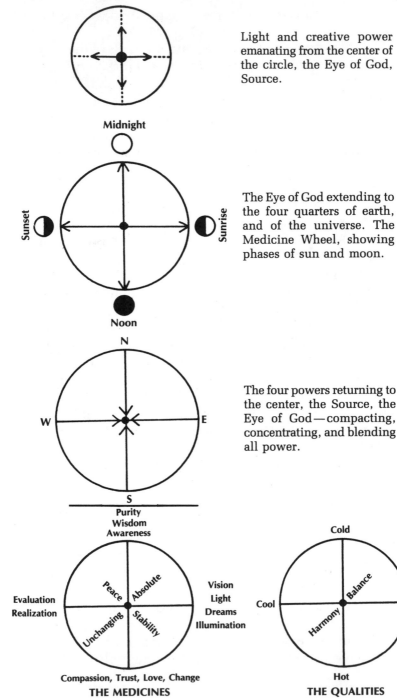

Light and creative power emanating from the center of the circle, the Eye of God, Source.

The Eye of God extending to the four quarters of earth, and of the universe. The Medicine Wheel, showing phases of sun and moon.

The four powers returning to the center, the Source, the Eye of God—compacting, concentrating, and blending all power.

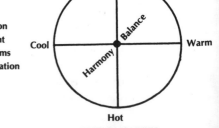

THE MEDICINES

THE QUALITIES

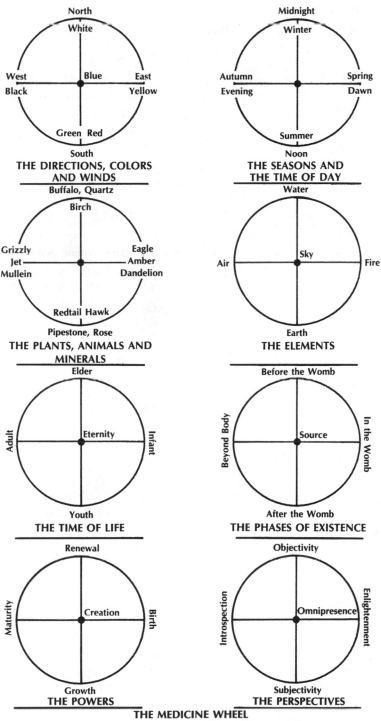

THE DIRECTIONS, COLORS
AND WINDS

THE SEASONS AND
THE TIME OF DAY

THE PLANTS, ANIMALS AND
MINERALS

THE ELEMENTS

THE TIME OF LIFE

THE PHASES OF EXISTENCE

THE POWERS

THE PERSPECTIVES

THE MEDICINE WHEEL
(TIME, PHASE, POWER AND PERSPECTIVE)

Our beginning place on the wheel depends on the season during which we were born. There are winter and summer people, autumn and spring people. There are spirit guides, spirit allies, spirit keepers, and totems. A spirit guide is with you for life in all circumstances, in all situations. A spirit ally assists you in specific situations and needs. Sometimes spirits are immaterial and live only in the spirit world, and sometimes they assume the form of living beings such as eagles and bears. A combination of these spirits with the medicine power of the season when a person was born is his totem, governed by the spirit keeper of that direction on the circle of life. For example, a person entering the wheel of life during winter is born with the medicine power of the North, and his totem combination is buffalo, aspen, and quartz crystal, governed by the spirit of the North.

One's totem forms the basis of his temperament and the power of his personality. One's guide, ally, and totem may be the same. My strongest guide in the protection and healing of myself and my people is also my totem, the grizzly.

I was born during autumn. My root strengths therefore are of the West, and my color is black. My first spirit guide was the spirit keeper of the West, the same as my totem. Besides the grizzly, my set of totems includes the medicine power of the mullein plant, jet, and the sunset. My power as a teacher and therapist stems from the qualities and perspective of this point on the wheel. These include healing oneself. The grizzly, more than any other animal, knows the ways of life and of earth to heal itself. The West also means teaching oneself through a process of developing authentic self-realization and awareness in the darkness (black) of introspection and inner evaluation. I use jet, my totem mineral, in protection from negativity and in counseling addicts. Jet neutralizes negativity.

Another quality of the West is taking honest inventory of one's own strengths, fears, and weaknesses. It is the power that comes from knowing oneself. Also autumn, the season of my birth, is a time of preparation. For myself and in guiding my students, I continually place strong emphasis on preparation. When I lead a sweat ceremony or guide a vision quest, those working with me know only too well that "the preparation is as important as the doing."

We are not limited to our beginning point on the wheel of life (as in the abuse of astrology). There is movement, change, addition, and expansion. The seasons change, the sun and moon have their phases. So, too, people journey on the odyssey of the medicine wheel in life's experiences and wanderings. Our totem is our beginning medicine power, given in grace at birth. Then our power expands in learning, tasks, and preparations, and we earn more power by renewing and sustaining previous visions and dreams. We receive a spirit guide or ally through the ordeal of the vision quest, which involves the preparations of sweat lodge purification, prayer, fasting, development of will, and self-discipline. We qualify by how we treat our human, plant, animal, and mineral relatives.

As I grew older and journeyed the wheel of life, other colors, plants, animals, powers, winds, and attributes of the wheel were added to my totem, as an expansion of my medicine power. As a result of vision quests, the golden eagle became a spirit guide; from several sun dances, the golden eagle also became a spirit ally. Through initiation into a warrior society, the redtail hawk became a spirit ally; initiation into a certain clan provided the phases of Grandmother Moon as powerful tools of self-realization and awareness. And the moon is always there wherever I go! So one's medicine power and consciousness can expand as we travel the wheel of life.

If we are not centered or balanced during our journey through change, our movement occurs through a series of crises instead of an even ebb and flow. Dangerous to ourselves and to others, we move lacking vision. Musical notes out of harmony produce noise, not music. The Medicine Wheel is movement and change in balance with ourselves, in harmony with others and with nature. Through it, we dance to the music of life's rhythm in nature, with Maheo as the conductor.

8
Medicine Wheel II:
Wisdom of the Four Directions

Each of the four Maheyuno or spirit keepers has a specific intelligence, and together they are known as the wisdom of the four directions. The Great Spirit Maheo is the source of wisdom and intelligence. All created things, spirit and matter, are images of Maheo and possess an intelligence of Source, which can be shared. When summoned, the wisdom and power of the four directions can be shared with human beings.

The Spirit of the East

The power of the East is the power of enlightenment, wisdom, and spiritual vision, our highest goals in life. It is the place of the morning star, the only star which shines with the sun. The medicine of the morning star is wisdom, involving the light of discernment. We Cheyennes are the Morning Star People, whose symbol is

This symbol provides the power of spiritual wisdom when contemplated as a mandala. One of our greatest chiefs was called Morning Star.

The season of the East is spring, the awakening of life from winter and the birth of new life, new seeds, new buds. It is a season of planting seeds and new ideas, new beginnings. The time is sunrise when life awakens from sleep. The colors are yellow and gold and have the power of invoking spiritual vision, growth, and healing. Yellow is the color of natural wisdom. With new life the universe is illuminated. So it is with the sunrise, which gives a special power to those who greet its rays. The time of life of the East is birth and infancy, the newborn, and its quality is innocence. The power of the East is that of light removing darkness, of a seed sprouting, and of a flower opening to the sun. It is a magnificent awakening, a new light, a new life.

The plant of the East is the dandelion, which is a source of vitamins A, B, and C. These help purify the blood. The mineral is amber, which is actually neither jewel nor mineral but the petrified tree resin of an extinct coniferous pine. Amber beads, amulets, and charms have been found in sites that date from ancient times. The ancients called it the ''tears of the sun, the perspiration of the earth.'' It is thousands of years old and contains the accumulated wisdom of the earth. As one of the most powerful healing agents in nature, it also contains the power of the sun.

Amber is used in ritual healing by shamans to invoke and embrace the healing powers. It contains elemental virtues and qualities useful in curing all sorts of disease. When mixed with honey and taken internally, amber has been prescribed for bad eyesight; worn externally it heals and protects the throat.

Light, the antagonist of darkness, the dispeller of

gloom and ignorance, is a great focus of healing. Amber irradiates light in a peculiarly pure way and is a source of wonder and inspiration. Amber glows yellow as the sun and is shaded light to dark, with a smooth silk-like luster. It is the gift to us from another healing agent, the wood of a tree.

Amber not only attracts light; it has electricity. Golden as the sun, charged with its hidden electrical power, it is a testimony that nothing ends, that life renews itself in countless ways. Yellow amber, once a tree growing in a long-ago forest, has changed form and become a different substance. In it is found the living embodiment of the Creative Spirit.

The animal of the East is the golden spotted eagle. It flies highest of all winged ones, thus closer to Maheo, and is the messenger of dreams and visions. The vision of the eagle from high places is like consciousness elevated, so the golden eagle is regarded as Maheo's messenger. It is the sun bird with feathers as rays of the sun. When any part of it is carried or worn, it represents the presence of God and of the higher self.

The spotted eagle corresponds to the Hindu idea of Buddhi, which is the intelligent consciousness of the formless, transcendent principle of all manifestation. Buddhi is expressed as being a ray directly emanating from Atma, the spiritual sun. We sing in some of our ceremonies, "The spotted eagle is coming to take me away." The eye of the eagle is the sun.

The Spirit of the South

The power of the South is growth occurring so rapidly that trust is needed because there may not be time for evaluation. It is a time of extending out into the world, experiencing and investigating. It is the time of testing ideas and methods, of putting knowledge, vision, and wisdom to work in the world.

The season is summer, when spring is fulfilled. The sun is direct and hot; there is movement and nature is flourishing. It is the time of the sun dance to celebrate and commune with earth and sun.

The power of the living, breathing earth is conspicuous at this time. The newborn of spring now experience the fast growth of the summer. The warm winds of the South embrace and nourish. Life is brought together. New projects are in process. The power of the South and of summer is the primal power of mating. The corresponding time of day is noon, and in human terms it represents youth. The colors are the red of the strong sun and the green of plants rapidly growing. Red is vitality and the passion of flowing life; green is the color of growth and trust. It is the color of earth, a balancing grounding color, neither hot nor cold. During rapid growth there are many changes and several lessons.

A mineral of the South is pipestone, a red clay-like stone, which is the petrified blood of the people mixed with the soil of Earth Mother. Its source is a sacred quarry whose history teaches a lesson in embracing peaceful tools, such as the sacred pipe, over weapons. Of all carving stone, pipestone is the most sacred for fashioning prayer pipes. It is also associated with the heart of the earth, the blood of the people, and the color of the strong sun.

The animal of the South is the redtail hawk, who likes the sun and warmth and is active and adaptable. It is a fearless hunter and swift flier. Often smaller birds attack this hawk but never cause it harm, a lesson to be applied in life. The color of its tail approximates the color of pipestone and reminds us of the Red Road. The tail of this hawk, the "red eagle," steers it in flight using the wind in harmony for balance. In our flight of life we are reminded to be continually steered on to the Red Road in harmony and balance.

The plant of this direction is the rose. The rose is a shrub with thorns which protect it only from those who would attempt to disturb it. As a strong source of vitamin C, it is used in remedies for sickness. Rosewater is used as a perfume and a hair rinse, as well as to invoke the medicine power of the South in ritual ceremony. The exchange of roses symbolizes love and trust.

My favorite rose is the wild rose, which ranges in color from light to bright pink. My grandmother had dried rose petals and pressed them between the pages of her Bible and of her journal. They were quite old. Pinches of them were given to us sometimes on special occasions. It was her request that these rose petals be buried with her. They were.

The Spirit of the West

The medicine power of the West and of autumn is introspection and self-evaluation, from which realization and awareness develop. The growth of summer stops, and during autumn life prepares for the season of renewal in the North during winter. The time is sunset, when most life prepares to slow down or sleep. So, too, humans contemplate and evaluate the lessons of growth. The West corresponds to our middle years, a time of harvesting ideas matured through testing, experimenting, and investigating in youth. Although fresh new visions never cease, this is when one should discover and develop strength to sustain visions already received and lessons already learned.

The medicine power of this direction and time is that of knowing oneself, in the darkness of solitude and introspection. Withdrawing from outside reality and journeying inward provides a mirror which reveals reflections otherwise unseen. Autumn is less intense yet a stronger time than summer; it is a time of preparation. Autumn represents the force of the spirit descending to earth, of material and physical experiences transformed into spiritual awareness and conclusions. Such is known as "Hyoka." In earlier times, Hyoka medicine was used by "contrary warriors" who mastered fighting techniques so well that they could perform them backwards! Hyoka medicine and contrary warriors are widely misunderstood and sensationalized. Hyoka can be compared to the Japanese koan and Chinese haiku; they express truth but don't make sense. Not all truth makes sense.

The color of the West is black, like the night. It is the color of withdrawing to the temple within to focus on the formlessness from which all things begin. Unfortunately, this color receives a lot of negative judgment and connotation, as in the term "black magic." This is an abuse and a distortion of the medicine power of the color black and a further misunderstanding of Hyoka. Satanism has no symbols of its own, no power unto itself. It uses twisted or upside-down symbols and images, taking life in its ceremonies instead of strengthening or giving life. It also thrives on fear and the abuse of power, with ego power goals taking precedence over soul power. Remember this and do not be afraid.

The ego can block the channel of the life spirit in us and restrict the flow of divine power. Fear acts as a wall between us and the Great Spirit. It is a blockage and a barrier. Most fears are shadows, without substance. You have enough divine power within yourself individually to cope with a hoard of satanists. To be convinced that white is good and black is bad is to be tricked by distorted thinking. Such is part of the lesson of black and of the West.

From the darkness of entering within comes new light. This seems contradictory; it is paradoxical and part of Hyoka medicine. There is a time when we should cease to gaze at the external multicolored reality and close our two eyes to the world, to view our inner qualities with the single intuitive eye of discernment.

An animal of the West is the grizzly bear which, like the color black, is also misunderstood. The lessons, power, and messages of the spirit of the West are not as straightforward as those of the South. They are Hyoka. Basically the grizzly is gentle and humorous when left alone hunting, sleeping, and frolicking in high mountain meadows. When threatened, it stands on two legs as a "two-legged"; it is the bear that "walks like a human." The vibration, intent, and power of a grizzly standing up is quite different from when it is walking on all fours. So, too, there are instances in our lives when we should stand tall. The grizzly is strong, yet gentle. Its silver tipped black hairs are as the stars in the night. There is a powerful medicine reason why the grizzly has a hump in its back, which I cannot share. Perhaps if you enter your wheel and journey to the West to reflect on the grizzly's hump, you will be told.

The grizzly knows the ways of life and the ways of spirit to heal itself more than any other animal in the forest. It is the chief of all spirit keepers, for without introspection, without inner direction, the lessons and powers of the other seasons of the wheel would appear less relevant to personal application.

There are other animals of the West, such as the raven and the thunderbird, which is the protector of the pipe and of all things sacred. Lightning, thunder, and hailstones are of the West. Hailstones represent several things all with much power. They are the spirit descending to earth, the transformation of physical experiences into spiritual conclusions. They are the white in the black; they are Hyoka. The priest Crazy Horse had hailstone medicine; his spirit guides were the shadow, the day, and the redbacked hawk. When Hyoka is mentioned, most folks reply, ''Oh, they are the contraries.'' That is only part of the power of Hyoka medicine. That is merely the visible surface of Hyoka.

The thunder beings travel and move around, but they originate and reside in the West. There are only two things I feel comfortable and respectful in sharing in writing about the thunder beings: they are always terrifying and they always bring good. They test you. They come inside the sweat lodge during ceremonies and sometimes come on a vision quest. During preparation for one of my first vision quests in my early twenties, a Chippewa medicine man assured me: ''Don't worry. If the thunder beings don't kill you, they'll make you stronger! You will either cross beyond into the spirit world, or you will remain in this world stronger. Both are good things.'' Yet somehow today when I pass that assurance on to some of my students pledging a vision quest, they don't seem relaxed and assured!

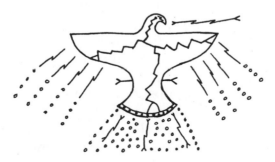

The stone of the West is jet, "black amber." Like amber it is a plant substance, the fossilized tree mulch of leaves and bark in water. The beauty of most jewels is in their capacity to reflect light, and this is one of the purposes of faceting precious stones. But jet and amber share their beauty in the radiations of light which emanate from inside them and in their soft, silky luster. Jet is not heavy, yet it is tough in texture. The spiritual application of this characteristic is obvious.

Jet is a protective substance used extensively by many ancient civilizations. It was carved into talismans, amulets, and tiny discs worn touching the skin. For the medicine of jet and the other minerals of the wheel, it is crucial to wear them on the body, touching the skin. It is not enough to possess a medicine object. A relationship must be formed involving a touching and a connecting, an invoking, and an embracing of the spirit power of the object in order for this power to be shared in an alliance. Some medicine objects may not be suitable for or compatible with one. Soul reflection and prayer for guidance are often required before a medicine object is used. This is more powerful than indiscriminate wishful thinking, because a wish is a desire without energy.

Jet contains the elements of earthly substances and many resinous purifying ingredients, which neutralize the power and spread of some kinds of germs. Powdered jet is burned in a fire to insure a safe return from journeys. A jet amulet neutralizes any negativity projected toward one from the world. It does so non-violently—it "neutralizes" negativity, it does not "destroy" it. This is big medicine. Like amber, jet can be ground to powder and burned. The fumes are beneficial in repelling germs and fever. Women in childbirth are given jet to hold. Powdered jet mixed with water is used as a paste for aching gums or toothaches and as a cleanser for teeth. Ointments or salves and powdered jet compounded with beeswax have therapeutic uses in the treatment of some skin disorders.

Jet is a black gem, a color associated with mourning and death, but there is nothing morbid or lacking in hope about jet. It holds within itself forces compounded of wood, earth, vegetable, and mineral substances, all active sources of protection, light, and healing.

Mullein is the plant of the West. Its leaves are made into a tea that helps liver problems and nervous conditions. The leaves are also smoked in pipes or burned as an incense. One of the many lessons of mullein is the important ability to be able to shift and change.

The time of life of the West is death, life beyond the earth without the physical body. The sun sets and the rays of the sun for the day are gone. The light of that day is over forever. This sounds so final. It is! This is why the day, the month, the season is not to be taken for granted. We have the guarantee of a new beginning, a new growth, a new dawn, with the rays of the sun returning at sunrise for a new day. It is sacred to grieve for a period over a death. Tears are strengthening and cleansing. But to embrace and cultivate unceasing grief or despair is to steal life, your life, and to hold back what you can fully share with those still living on this earth plane of existence with you.

Death is transition. It is a change. It is a return. Death is "an" end, it is not "the" end. My dog Cheena passed over recently. He was with me for thirteen years. He was not a pet, he was my brother. As we buried him, I could not speak the words I had written about him. My throat was frozen silent in sorrow. My experiences with this four-legged flashed before my consciousness as slides in a projector. My heart seemed as a lead block. I felt almost angry that he was taken. But the memory of his death, his act of dying, was medicine for me. Cheena left his body at my doorstep (where he lived) with his head facing West, exactly at sunset, on a new moon, in autumn. I smiled in strength and hoped my death would be as harmonious with nature.

I thanked the Great Spirit for allowing us to spend time together on Earth Mother under Blue Sky Father. The powers of the universe were thanked for the blessing of Cheena's presence among us for thirteen years. I gave thanks for what I was given and did not get angry for what was taken. One of my spirit guides told me Cheena may or may not return to earth in a different form. I am keeping my eyes open. I will know if he comes.

This is what I wrote about my brother-dog Cheena:

MOGWA CHEENA

Alias "Big Boy, Good Boy, Wart Hog"

1972 - 1985

The best dog I ever had.

The best dog I shall ever have.

Raised in the mountains of the North,

You shadowed me through the West,

and the southwest.

You made my days.

Perhaps we will meet again,

Until then, so long, Big Boy.

The Spirit of the North

The medicine power of the North is renewal and purity; its quality is objectivity. As there is a time of withdrawing from the external world and entering within oneself, there also is a time, a cycle, of withdrawing and rising above our multicolored, multidimensional reality to view our life in objectivity, for cleansing and renewal. This time of life is old age, which I prefer to call "elderhood." At this time we are slowed down in the things of the world but are quickened in spirit. So, too, are the Earth Mother and the animals of the forest. Think of the difference between water, steam, and ice.

The season of this direction is winter, when the earth seems to be asleep. The time of day is midnight, when we are in rest from the day. Life and the forces of nature renew themselves in sleep for the coming new growth of spring. As the snow falls, it covers the multicolored forms of existence with a white blanket. A walk in the snow is fresh, vitalizing, and crisp. The animals are either asleep or are ready to move out with a renewed vitality. Leaves are gone; seeds are dormant yet very much alive. As snow melts in spring, it reveals that which was hidden, a fresh, vital new growth.

This time in life and position on the wheel is sometimes difficult. The winter appears stark, naked, cold, harsh, barren. It is a time of testing, a time to clean up one's behavior—a time of purification. The color is white for purity, for snow, for ice, and the color of changing hair as it ages. Too many of us view purity as being self-righteous or holier-than-thou. Purity is a concentration and compaction of power. In the dogma and doctrine of man-made religion, purity is associated with judgment. In the natural order of the universe, purity is essential for renewal and new growth, for integrity and clarity of perception to sustain and maintain previous visions and dreams. As we become elders, we are potential sources of counsel for the young. We pass on our stories, experiences, and wisdom to catalyze the growth of others. Such a sacred responsibility requires purity, clarity and objectivity to be a source of clear light for others. The quality of one's consciousness in old age is a testimony to his personal evolution and growth.

The northern winter time of life focuses on spiritual values. We become not so much retired from life as we are consultants, still there, still doing, "in" the world but no longer "of" the world. This is a valuable principle, not exclusive to this time of life and position on the wheel of life, though it is concentrated there.

The mineral of the North is quartz crystal, capable of elevating consciousness. It is the sacred ice mineral. The plants are birch and aspen. The animal is the white buffalo, strong, mystical, physically as well as spiritually nourishing to the people. The Great Spirit often assumes the form of the white buffalo. The wisdom of the North is a distilled wisdom, a wisdom distinct from the natural wisdom of the East. In this time and place in life, we can be in union with the medicine power of the white buffalo, being as a sacred messenger to the people. The gift of the sacred pipe came out of the North through White Buffalo Calf Maiden to the Sioux and to some other Plains tribes.

Often the lessons of winter and the North are referred to as "the cold winds of objective truth." Some truths of the experiences occurring in our life, with its relationships, attitudes, and priorities, may not always appear pleasant when viewed through the pure, renewed eye of objectivity. But such is essential if we are to see the forest as well as the trees. Purity, renewal, and objectivity require time, effort, and patience. So does creativity. Memories of my winters in Montana, watching the snow pile higher against the cabin window, remind me of the value and power and blessing of not being able to go anywhere, of not being distracted by outside events, of time that seems to stand still. Folks are pushed closer together, deeper into themselves. Relationships are tested. Situations are dealt with. Patience may wear thin, revealing feelings that should no longer remain suppressed or hidden.

Many of my students express to me that they would like to get snowed in at a cabin in Montana. Well, this is one of the reasons for the Medicine Wheel. We can journey to the power and realization of this "direction" in life anywhere, any time, by setting up a wheel. But there is the student who retorts, "Well, I'll set up the wheel outside a cabin in Montana!"

Purity is essential in preparation, but winter is a time of renewal, for preparation for the upcoming spring. The Medicine Wheel and its medicine power cannot be pigeonholed. It is circular, not linear. Its focus is on the importance of process beyond product. A student or seeker may confront me: "But you said autumn was 'the' time of preparation." Autumn is "a" time of preparation. Each season, each lesson learned, is a preparation for the next. The predominant force of the North is the power of purity and renewal. Purification is necessary before other things can be attempted or learned. Purification sensitizes and focuses one's perception. The rite of purification in the sweat lodge is performed before most ceremonies and undertakings can occur. Smudging of one's body and lodge with cedar and sweet grass is an act of purification before medicine bundles are opened, before the pipe is smoked, and it precedes many other sacred doings. Medicine objects are regularly smudged for purification and renewal. A person's vision and guidance from the invisible world must be kept pure and renewed, so that they will remain strong, vivid, clear, and not cluttered with ego or wishful thinking.

Prior to my initiation as a ceremonial leader, I was told by one of my instructors that I was carrying the pipe and ceremonies in one hand and all sorts of things in my other hand. The "things" in one hand or the other had to be released. There would be no judgment as to which things would be released—the choice was mine. My understanding of this request was incomplete, yet I sensed my instructor was presenting me the cold winds of objective truth from the North. So I went out alone, set up my wheel, and sat in the North contemplating his request. In a short time it was revealed to me that there were certain attitudes, behaviors, and other things in my life that had to be either changed or released if I was to continue as a pipeholder with possible growth transformation into a ceremonial priest. In time, using the Medicine Wheel, I changed. I released. I grew. I was transformed by the renewing and the purifying of my spirit. I recall the sacred scripture. ''Be yet not consumed, rather transformed by the renewing of your spirit.'' This is the wisdom and power of the Spirit of the North.

9

Medicine Wheel III:
Setting Up and Using the Wheel

I will explain the use and setup of the Medicine Wheel, but be prudent and cautious. Do not use it lightly. Always remember that the power of the circle of the wheel is in the doing, not the telling. Such is the truth of all ceremony, of all medicine tools.

It is good to smudge yourself before setting up a wheel. Smudging is using smoke for purification. Cedar smoke clears away negativity, and sweet grass smoke attracts positive energy and attracts spirits. I don't encourage people to rush into getting pipes and doing ceremonies. I do, however, suggest to all seekers of nature to learn appropriate smudging and the use of the Medicine Wheel. If you do nothing else, assemble your Medicine Wheel bundle. This is your basic spiritual tool kit, as well as your guide to growth and your vehicle of travel on the Medicine Road. My students of the Red Road learn their wheel before anything else. It is the epitome of preparation. The wheel assists you in any direction you wish to travel, and it also transcends direction. The wheel can take you within yourself into the lake of self-realization, or to the sea of the Creator in divine communion. It can assist you in communicating with animals, learning the secrets of plants, and the hidden wisdom of rocks, or in resolving relationships with others.

But the wheel is not a cure-all. It is not "the" tool; it is "a" tool. The Creative Spirit is acknowledged and respected in all life, yet only Source itself, only the Creator, is worshipped. To worship a favorite tool or a responsive spirit guide or ally is to create a false idol. Be prudent. Be cautious. Be patient. Use the wheel to learn the wheel. Above all, remember that nature and the Medicine Wheel are circular, not linear. Bear witness to your experiences and the experiences of others. Don't judge them, or you will lose power. Don't give away your power to any belief, any teacher. Get beyond your mind, unlock your heart, fan the spark of your soul intuition into flame, and go for it!

Instructions to Make a Wheel

Constructing a Medicine Wheel is a ceremony that acknowledges the divine Creator. It should be done reverently but also with joy and a sense of ease.

To begin, find five wooden pegs or stones. Pray over them and smudge them with cedar and sweet grass. Paint them or tie colored ribbons on them. The center peg or stone is blue for Blue Sky Father. Paint or ribbon each of the remaining four to correspond to the colors of the four directions: the East is yellow, the South is red or green, the West is black, and the North is white.

First find the center and mark it with the blue peg. Raise the blue peg toward the sky and extend it down to earth; then stake it into the ground where you want the center of your wheel. Take seven or four steps from the center to the East and stake the eastern peg. The beginning of the wheel is the East. Always enter and leave the wheel through the East. After staking the East, return to the center. Take the same number of steps toward the South and stake the southern peg. Return to the center. Take the same number of steps from the center to the West and stake the western peg. Return to the center. Take the same number of steps from the center to the North and stake the northern peg. Return to the center. You have now marked the four cardinal points. When moving about in the wheel between the cardinal points, always pass through the center. Discover for yourself the meaning of always passing through the center when changing the direction of movement.

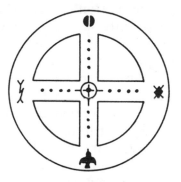

Your wheel is now set up. Don't step across the circumference boundary of the wheel. When entering or leaving it, do so only through the East. You may leave your wheel after it is set up. A wheel can be set up temporarily for specific use or left set up for a long time. If setting it up for a long period, use large rocks instead of portable pegs.

You may bring someone into your wheel with you. But I suggest you don't do so indiscriminately and that you familiarize yourself with the wheel first. This is a sacred tool, not to be used as a game to impress

friends. But relax in it. Do not be intimidated by its
power and sacredness. Be reverent and comfortable.
Feel the peace of the circle and its center.

Choose one direction where you want to spend time,
or choose the center. Go there and get comfortable,
sitting, standing, or lying down. Say the name of the
direction at which you are located. Close your eyes
and take seven deep breaths, filling your abdomen,
lower chest, and upper chest with air, inhaling
through your nose. Exhale with your mouth releasing air in succession from upper chest, lower chest,
and abdomen. Do this seven times. Then just listen
to the sound of your breath for a while. Let your breath
breathe at its own pace. Don't try to slow it if it is fast.
As you inhale, mentally say "earth"; as you exhale,
mentally say "sky." Inhaling is the taking in, the re-
ceptive, the acceptance of life, the Mother. Exhaling
is the releasing, the active, the transcendence, the
Father. Listen to your breath and chant "sky," "earth"
for about ten minutes. Your own breath will calm you
without contrived effort to relax.

Using your will (your individual volition is the dy-
namo feeding your power), withdraw the energy of
your senses from the external world. Collect this
energy, concentrate it, and focus it at the point on the
wheel where you are: North, South, East, West, or center. You are connecting with the medicine power of
that part of the Medicine Wheel. After a while—you
will know when—cease focusing on the direction and
remain still and silent. Listen and perceive the power
of the direction you seek. It may manifest itself as
light, color, sound, insight, or in another way. Open
and close your eyes periodically. Be attentive.

In time you may want to move about among the four
directions. Always pass through the center. You may

want to examine a problem or an idea as viewed from the perspective and power of each direction. You may be so confused or upset that you wish to spend time only in the center.

The Medicine Wheel is a tool of self-realization and divine communion. It may be used to examine a relationship with a mate, to evaluate a career decision, to resolve a financial problem, to face the Great Mystery and its four spirit keepers, or for many other purposes.

When you are ready, you may take down your wheel ceremonially. First, remove the eastern peg; go through the center and remove the southern peg; go through the center and remove the western peg; go through the center and remove the northern peg; and then go to the center and pull up the center peg. The center peg is the first one staked and last one pulled up. Of the pegs at the cardinal points, the eastern one is always first to be staked and first to be pulled up, thus completing the clockwise (direction of the sun) circles. Your movement is then in accord with nature: spring preceding summer, etc.

If you do nothing but set up a wheel and sit in it, this is power. The act of constructing a wheel is power. It is a spiritual exercise and gradually develops your power and will. Be patient and persistent. Be attentive.

Permanent Medicine Wheels

I have attended ceremonies in which nearly a hundred people were in a wheel. Some Medicine Wheels up north are quite large and the rocks forming them are still there. There are the remnants of a wheel in Wyoming with a diameter of approximately 200 feet. There is a permanent Medicine Wheel erected around the 600-acre ranch we call home. There are ten-foot forked poles for each of the four directions. Our ceremonial tipi and sweat lodge and dwellings are at the center. We live in a Medicine Wheel.

When folks come out here for counseling or preparing for a vision quest, they travel the Medicine Wheel with me. In counseling, a session may happen at any one of the four directions. This is using the medicine power of the circle and the forces of nature in partnership with my professional training in psychology. It is a blending of mind and soul with spirit and nature.

The Prayer Pipe and the Medicine Wheel

The power of the Great Spirit descends among us in the forces of nature and in the invisible spirit world. The power of the Great Spirit in us ascends as our consciousness expands and rises. In ancient times the idea of these forces was conveyed by the symbol of a tree and later by the symbols of the pipe and medicine wheel.

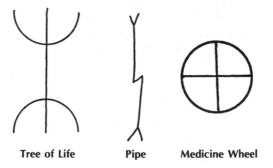

Tree of Life   Pipe   Medicine Wheel

These invisible forces from the Great Spirit are a source of power and energy. Life is sustained by contact with them. The pipe and the Medicine Wheel are tools for obtaining contact with them and for main-

The West

The South

The Medicine Wheel ceremonial circle

taining harmony and balance between the power within us and the forces among us. The symbols of the pipe and wheel express our relationship to earth and sky. The forces in nature have been called "angels" by some ancient tribes. These tribes not only knew of these forces but had specific methods of contacting and using them. The forces were given names such as Gabriel and Michael. Among North American tribes these powers are known as spirit keepers, spirit guides, or allies. The symbolic tree of life, pipe, and Medicine Wheel illustrate how we are all inseparably interconnected to all earthly and heavenly forces, and these symbols show our relationship to each.

The tree of life enables us to understand how we are surrounded by forces of the visible world of nature and the invisible "cosmic" world. The Medicine Wheel and the pipe guide us in how to enter into communion with these forces and powers, how to use them in our bodies and consciousness. The purposes of communing with nature and the Great Spirit are:

To make us conscious of its aspects and activities.

To make us aware of centers within us that can receive currents of its energy.

To establish a connection between us, nature, and Source, in harmony and balance.

The Cause of Evil

Communing with nature and with the Great Spirit requires spiritual exercise, purification, and the development and use of will. Communing points the way to freedom, the way of liberation from a fragmented and alienated view of nature, and also from being powerless to negative conditions, either in body, mind, or spirit. The forces of nature and the powers within us are manifestations of positive, superior energy from the Great Spirit. Human beings—by our deviations from the order, harmony, balance and wisdom of these superior forces—create negative inferior forces that can accumulate and intensify. Present-day despair and illness are caused by our current deviations from the natural law, order, and harmony with natural and cosmic forces. These are deviations in thinking, feeling, and acting. Lack of will power is directly related to loss or giving away of one's medicine power, through dispersion of energy, laziness, unrestrained indulgences, or disease.

The individual soul was created as an extension of the Great Spirit. It is a reflection of God's consciousness. The soul is light which evolves and matures into the likeness of the Great Spirit, just as a seed becomes a tree. The visions of some shamans and elders reveal that there is no intrinsic evil, that the nature of everything is the soul, which is perfect goodness. Beings act evilly when they abuse power and consequently lose touch with their soul. Negative energy and evil actions can accumulate and intensify; the vicious circle of negative behavior is an example of the abuse of the power of the circle. However, the circle itself is beautiful; negative behavior is an abuse of a good thing.

The story of Satan illustrates the lessons of this abuse, the deviation from the good, the beautiful. Originally Satan was Lucifer, a very beautiful manifestation of the invisible power of God. Instead of evolving and transforming into a higher state by the renewing of his spirit, he was held in a spell by the illusion of his own beauty. Lucifer took the glory of the Source of his beauty unto himself. He ceased to acknowledge Source. Pride completely replaced humility and devotion. This was his "fall"; such is the downfall of those following Lucifer's trail. The lesson of Lucifer's behavior further reveals that such a path is fire and pain (hell) instead of light and peace (heaven).

Pipe Ceremony

In smoking the sacred pipe, we share breath and commune with all creation and its power and forces. During a pipe ceremony people in a circle commune with one another by sharing breath. Each becomes all. There is a spiritual power in everything, in each of us. It is called *Ch'i* by the Chinese, *Ki* by the Japanese, *prana* by the Indian yogis, *Ruach* by the Hebrew prophets, *Ruh* by the Sufi saints, *pneuma* by the Greeks, and *medicine* by many Native Americans. The English word "spirit" is derived from the Latin "spiritus." In all these languages and diverse cultures, the word "spirit" relates to breath. In most cases the same word is used for both. The Holy Spirit to the Jewish mystics is the "Ruach Elohim," the Breath of God. Among Cheyennes, spirit is called "Matasooma."

By taking our pipe in the Medicine Wheel, we share breath with all of the four major powers of the universe. We enter into communion with each spirit guide by sharing spirit (breath) through the sacred pipe, and we offer breath (life) in ceremonious acknowledgments to celebrate and to connect with the wisdom and power of that position of the wheel. The natural result of such communion is insight, comfort, assurance, and power. Peace and joy become perceived experiences instead of abstract concepts. The value of beautiful abstract concepts can never be ignored. But there must be a point at which they are transformed into the medicine of perceived experience. The power of the pipe and the wheel is experiential; these sacred tools simply must be used by doing.

There are many ways the sacred pipe is used in combination with the Medicine Wheel. When the pipe is customarily offered to Earth Mother, Sky Father, and the four directions, the four spirit guides are summoned to bear witness to the prayer and to offer their guidance and blessing. In this manner, an invisible wheel is constructed.

Sometimes when in a traffic jam or while waiting in long lines or in a business office, I mentally construct a wheel and travel in it. You may wish to do this while flat on your back in a sick bed. You may want mentally to set up a wheel of protection around you when you are in danger or immediately after an accident or while you are "clashing horns" with another during an argument. Years ago I mentally set up a Medicine Wheel around me before I attended a courtroom hearing regarding the use of peyote as a legal sacrament. These uses of the wheel are appropriate. Such use is self-realization and the exercise of personal will power. This is not superstition or manipulation. It is the harmony of logic, reason, intuitive wisdom, and individual will with the will of the ultimate reality—God.

Traditionally, when in a Medicine Wheel, one takes the sacred pipe. But the use of the Medicine Wheel is not dependent upon a pipe. Each of us individually is a living, breathing pipe. Our head is the bowl, our spine is the stem.

The phases of the sun and moon, as well as the changing of the seasons of the year, can be acknowledged and celebrated with the sacred pipe in the Medicine Wheel. This past autumn equinox we celebrated the passing of the spirit of summer and the arrival of the spirit of autumn with a pipe ceremony in the wheel. We began at the center of the wheel and offered smoke with the pipe to the earth and sky and summoned the four spirit keepers. We took the sacred pipe to the southern point in the wheel and offered smoke, thanking summer for its lessons, guidance, and powers. Some had specific thanksgivings for personal blessings and sacred events of that previous summer. We bid summer farewell.

Then we passed back through the center of the wheel and journeyed to the western point. We offered smoke to the spirit of autumn and welcomed its return from last year. We expressed our hopes and aspirations for the upcoming autumn. Then we sat with the pipe, in silent contemplation of autumn. Prayer involves listening in silence as well as speaking. So we sat for awhile to listen to the force and power of the spirit of autumn, of the West.

One must be attentive. A visible manifestation may occur. An inner perception or insight may be revealed from one's higher self (the intelligence of the soul). During this ceremony, for example, some coyotes started barking and howling, and the wind shifted and began blowing directly from the West. The coyote is one of the animals of the South. Perhaps this was the South (summer) bidding us farewell until next year, and the west wind announcing its arrival and presence. Some spiritual signs are immediately grasped, while others must be carefully examined with the discriminating eye of intuition (the Shanta Ista) in reflective silence.

After this autumn equinox ceremony, we traveled to the western pole in our larger permanent wheel and tied a new black ribbon to it. Faded black ribbons from ceremonies of previous years danced in the western breeze beneath the bright new ribbon. I then gave an offering with a pinch of tobacco, and spoke to my son about how the guidance of the West could be applied in his life. This is one of the ways in which the sacred pipe is used with the Medicine Wheel.

Entering into the circle of life with breath is very sacred. The two main approaches to the uses of the sacred pipe and the Medicine Wheel are at the two levels of Native Indian experience mentioned earlier: acceptance and transcendence. There are times when we use these sacred tools to become more involved in this world; there are times we use them to leave this world, to travel to other worlds. At such a time there is the act of devotion and sending prayers upward in the smoke, to the four primary aspects and activities of the Great Spirit, the four directions, the four winds, the four quarters of the circle of the universe.

A Farewell Ceremony

My friend and warrior society brother Will Sun came up from southern New Mexico last year to spend winter solstice and earth renewal (December 20 through 22) out on the land with us. He is a Lakota Sioux brother I worked with counseling inmates at the New Mexico State penitentiary, and I also helped him on his vision quest, his sun dance, and in preparing his pipe bundle. Although our relationship began years ago as that of student and instructor, he has since grown and flourished as a traditional pipeholder, sweat lodge ceremony leader, and was initiated recently as a warrior brother in the Redtail Hawk Medicine Society. Will is often a consultant and assistant to me during instruction and ceremonies. He is a man without vanity and represents the classic example of the instructor's student becoming the instructor's teacher. This is the finest testimony and compliment a student can give a teacher.

During his time with us at the ranch over winter solstice and earth renewal, Will was in complete harmony with the purifying and renewing powers of the season of winter and the point of North on the Medicine Wheel of life. After a sweat lodge ceremony, Will shared that he was in love with a woman whose natural life style was that of a mountain woman. She was called Elk Woman. I told Will that a large part of elk medicine among northern Indians involved "love dreaming" medicine, that people known as "elk dreamers" used elk medicine to deal with love and matters of the heart. Will told me that he was "no elk dreamer but that he was dreaming about Elk Woman!"

Will also explained that Elk Woman fell in love with her old boyfriend and was moving out of Will's house to return to him. A tradition among many tribes is for a man to give a pipe away when his woman leaves him for another, often to the man his woman chooses to leave him for. This tradition is voluntarily embraced and is by no means mandatory (thank goodness the Great Spirit is kind and merciful!). It was Will's wish to give Elk Woman a pipe, instruct her about its use, bless her, and send her to her boyfriend with a good heart. Will wanted to make the pipe he would give her. His request of me was to teach him how to make a pipe. I agreed to do so.

During the days of the winter solstice and earth renewal period, Will spent much time in the Medicine Wheel we had set up—where the tipi usually is at other times of the year. Its four points were marked by painted wood stakes. He would sit at each of the four directions to contemplate the situation about Elk Woman and her boyfriend. Some mornings Will would spend time in the South. Some evenings he would sit in the center. Upon entering the Medicine Wheel, whose symbol was drawn in the dirt, he would always bow first and enter through the East. He would also exit the wheel through the East.

During those days I instructed and guided Will

through the making and completion of his first pipe. Each step of the process involved prayer and the smudging of one's body, tools, equipment, and work area with the cleansing power of the smoke from burning cedar leaves. Often sweet grass is also burned to "bring in" the power of spirit. Will used the Medicine Wheel as a tool for concentrating and focusing his mind while working on the pipe, as well as using it as a tool to develop personal detachment and release of Elk Woman.

Within a week Will finished a beautiful stone pipe with an ash stem. He inlaid the bowl with silver and decorated the stem with beadwork and hanging twisted fringe. He invited Elk Woman up to the ranch and presented the pipe to her inside the Medicine Wheel. Then we also had a Medicine Wheel ceremony to dedicate and bless her new pipe. Elk Woman's pipe was taken to each of the four directions in the wheel and prayed over, then it was placed on a buffalo skull altar at the center of of the wheel. We sat in silent prayer and contemplation. Will then gave Elk Woman a blanket and told her that if he could not be with her to keep her warm, then the blanket would keep her warm.

This ceremony using the Medicine Wheel represented the giveaway of Will's attachment and possessiveness toward Elk Woman. Will and Elk Woman were made stronger by the resolving of a seemingly touchy situation. The Medicine Wheel was ceremoniously used to deal with a relationship between a man and woman on a spiritual level, above jealousy and malcontent. Elk Woman returned to her boyfriend in peace with a pipe and with a story to tell him about a Red Road warrior's love for her and his choice not to detain her but to bid her farewell with love and in peace.

10

The Pipe and a Last Good-Bye

One summer just before Indian market in August, my neighbor and friend Tavlos, an artist of Santa Fe, asked me to come with my pipe and say prayers at his wife's funeral. She had passed over after dealing with a terminal disease for a long time. I told him I would be there near sunset.

My heart was heavy as I drove over the hills and through the countryside to Tavlos's house northwest of Sante Fe. I had just finished dedicating and blessing a new prayer pipe that summer because I had given away my pipe to a family at the Taos Pueblo for their nephew's coming-of-age ceremony. Little did I know when I dedicated my new pipe to the Great Spirit during a solar eclipse, that one of the first ceremonies I would be requested to perform with it would be at a funeral.

I stopped atop a hill overlooking Tavlos's house and got out of my truck. The hot New Mexico sun was descending closer to the Western horizon and provided a glowing red backdrop for a flock of bluebirds. I burned some cedar and smudged myself with its smoke to cleanse myself of any negative energy lingering in or on me from that day's mundane activities.

Then I burned some sweet grass and inhaled its sweet
aroma, to attract spirit power to assist and to guide
me in that which I was called upon to do.

Suddenly, without warning, tears fell from my eyes.
I knew Tavlos's wife; she was a beautiful frail little
sister. I cannot mention her name because to do so
would be to call her back from her journey beyond
Se'han (the Milky Way) to the Great Spirit. I used to
hide in the bushes with my son Trinity and watch her
fill jugs with water from our well at the ranch. She
and Tavlos preferred the sweet taste of well water to
city water.

One evening that previous winter, at dinner with
a group of friends, I sat next to her and flirted with
her. Her grace and beauty was as the natural elegance
of a blue heron. It was cold that night and she was
feeling the chill strongly because of her sickness. But
she was a strong little warrior sister; she never com-
plained and was in good spirits. I told her that winter
night that I would like to make a medicine necklace
for her, that it would be an honor for me to do so. Her
face gleamed in delight as she told me that she would
love a "Freesoul necklace." But she cautioned me that
I shouldn't wait too long to get it to her. I understood
her innuendo. She knew her death was near. She and
Tavlos had talked about it and prepared for it at home
in the country, in the house they loved and built together. She was young—in her twenties. She was full
of life and humor; she loved life, yet was ready to face
death unafraid. I was amazed that her relaxed attitude
and pleasant humor that night was not contrived but
genuine and full of light. Her bright countenance sitting next to me at dinner lifted me from a deep melan-
choly in which I had been lingering the previous day.

In the following months that winter, she and I
would pass one another regularly driving back and

forth to town on Tano Road. She would smile and wave, always happy to see me drive by. Each time I saw her I would remind myself that I had to get over and visit her and bring her the necklace I had promised. That year was compulsively frantic for me in that I did ten major gallery shows in twelve months. I never went over to give her the necklace. Now, as I stood on that hill overlooking her house, she was gone. Her funeral finally brought me to her. The tear drops beneath my eyes now flowed steadily as streams down my face.

I lifted my arms and extended my pipe upward toward the sky, to Sky Father. I had to pray and breathe deeply to deal with my grief and to get centered before I could come off that hill and console my friend Tavlos. Others would be there too, friends and relatives waiting for me to arrive with the sacred pipe, to pray over the body of a sister whose spirit was now free from sickness and pain. I asked Sky Father to help this weeping warrior, to give him the strength to carry his heavy heart to this sacred pipe ceremony. Soon I had a vision. I saw myself counseling folks grieving over a death in their family, as I have done many times. I watched myself speak to them. I could not hear what I was saying, but I saw my lips moving, and the people seemed to feel better and become stronger as I spoke. This vision of myself counseling grieving people consoled me and gave me strength. I touched my pipe to my forehead and to the ground and thanked the Great Spirit for his guiding strength that came through a vision of my higher self. The sound of my own voice above me and descending down, as if echoing through a tunnel, told me that the sun was about to set and that it was time to go down from the hill and smoke the pipe with Tavlos at his wife's funeral. I sang out loudly to the four directions, "Hetchetou-alou," so be it!

When I arrived at Tavlos's house, there was a small group of about ten people including some of his wife's relatives. Tavlos greeted me and thanked me for coming because he wanted a pipe ceremony that day. Tavlos's eyes were deep with feeling and grief, but he was centered. He smiled and told me that it was time for her to go, that he was up all night with her, that she had helped prepare for her own death. He led me to the room where his wife's body lay, wrapped completely in white cloth, with flower petals sprinkled over her. Hanging above and beneath her body were brightly colored blue and red blankets with embroidered eastern religious symbols. The room was filled with many lighted candles. The smoke from sandalwood incense permeated the air and descended in an ethereal haze. A large picture window faced the West, and the setting sun could be seen in full panoramic view as if on a large video screen.

As I knelt down on the floor in front of her body, I could hear people slowly entering the room behind me. I opened my pipe bundle and held the pipe bowl in my left hand and its stem in my right hand. Raising both arms upward and over her body, I prayed for Grandfather Great Spirit to send Sky Father and Earth Mother to witness this sacred pipe ceremony. I then joined pipe bowl and stem together in sacred union. After sprinkling some tobacco on her body, I loaded the pipe, lit it, and offered smoke to each of the four directions. I sat the pipe down on the floor between me and her body with its stem facing the West. The sun's last rays disappeared behind the western horizon. In the prayer that sunset, we two-legged humans accepted the passing over of our sister's spirit, and acknowledged that her life was not over but changed. We bid her farewell as she traveled away from us across the Milky Way to the spirit world. We did not know much about the spirit world she was entering, but we did know that she did not need her body where she was going, as she had left it behind, perhaps as a reminder that she was among us for awhile.

We thanked the Great Spirit for allowing us to travel the Red Road of life on the earth plane for awhile with her, promising that we would not complain that our time with her was short and that she had died young. We bore witness to the fact that the setting sun and the western point on the Medicine Wheel of life represented death, the passing of light into darkness, but that death was not "the end" but "an end," that death was a change. There is always the promise of the light of a new sunrise after every sunset has passed.

I turned and faced Tavlos and told him that his relationship with his wife had not ended, that it now had changed, that his wife's spirit was no longer confined in a weak body. Now she could travel with him anywhere, any time. I picked up the pipe, lit it, inhaled and then exhaled sacred smoke over her body. I then turned and faced Tavlos again and exhaled sacred smoke towards him. I told Tavlos and the people present to remember this day, not in grief, but as a reminder and testimony that the sun both rises and sets on life, not to cherish one above the other, that life and death are different points on the circle of existence. I could see in their eyes that they understood.

Then I turned again and faced her body. With one hand I held my pipe and with the other I took a necklace from my pocket and held it over her body. I told her that she did not completely escape me, that in being requested to come today with the sacred pipe, I had a last chance to bring her necklace, as I had promised. I gently laid it on her body next to her heart. I thanked her for letting me flirt with her that previous winter at dinner. I told her she raised my spirits that evening. I bid her farewell and explained that I would never let my sadness become so heavy as to burden her travel away from nature to spirit.

I then offered the pipe to the four directions and pointed its stem toward the West for awhile, to thank the spirit guardian of the West for its blessings and lessons. I then extended it, stem first, down toward earth and then upward toward sky. The sacred pipe ceremony for the funeral of Tavlos's wife was now complete.

Tavlos had food prepared for a quiet "celebration" of the passing on of a sweet warrior woman. I did not stay for it. I went home and spent the rest of that evening alone, walking out on the prairie towards the North, the point of the Medicine Wheel of life that holds the cold winds of objective truth, those truths of life which are often unpleasant but nonetheless beautiful and real. Although it was a summer night, I felt a cold chill as I walked. I remembered my father telling me as a child that when a spirit leaves its body, its departure can be felt among the living as a chilly breeze.

III
Walking the Red Road Today

Do not misunderstand me, but understand me fully with reference to my affection for the land. I never said the land was mine to do with it as I chose.

The one who has the right to dispose of it is the one who has created it. I claim a right to live on my land, and accord you the privilege to live on yours.

CHIEF JOSEPH

11

Recent Days among the Cheyenne and Arapahoe

$\sim$

Originally the state of Oklahoma was known as Indian territory, for it was here that several Indian tribes were relocated by the United States Government after their defeat or surrender. The Cheyenne and Arapahoe tribes lived together most of the time and performed many ceremonies together; they are affiliated tribes. The Arapahoe was about the most peaceful of Plains tribes, known as peacemakers between warring tribes. It was the Arapahoes who were instrumental in the great peace made between the Cheyennes and Kiowas in the early 1800s. The Arapahoes were nicknamed "The Blue Cloud" people. The Cheyenne call themselves "Tsisistas" (human beings) or the Morning Star people. I am proud to be a Cheyenne-Arapahoe Indian.

Some Cheyenne-Arapahoes were sent to Darlington agency in Oklahoma Indian territory. Others were sent to prison at Fort Marion in Florida. Those still fighting became known as the "hostiles" or the "northerners," because they refused to relocate and leave their original homeland in Montana and Colorado. Consequently, today we have the northern Cheyenne-Arapahoe and the southern Cheyenne-Arapahoe comprising the Cheyenne-Arapahoe Nation. After 1874, some Cheyenne-Arapahoes (southerners) were relocated to Seger Colony, founded by John H. Seger. There he started the Seger Indian School. Later, Seger Colony became the town of Colony, Oklahoma. Many Cheyennes and Arapahoes grew to trust John Seger because he always respected them and learned their ways.

Colony is located about seventy-five miles southwest of Oklahoma City between Weatherford and Anadarko. It is a small town with one gas station, a restaurant, an old-time general store, and a post office. The Seger Indian School buildings still remain, about three blocks from the center of town. This old Seger Indian School site is the place of the annual traditional Cheyenne-Arapahoe powwow each Labor Day weekend.

It was the grand opening of the Gallery of the Plains Indian by Yvonne Kauger and her family that brought me to Colony to connect with my southern Cheyenne-Arapahoe relatives. I am a Cheyenne-Arapahoe from Missoula, Montana. Yvonne's father, John Kauger, lived in Colony all his life and raised his family among the Cheyenne-Arapahoe. They respect and accept him as a relative. They adopted his daughter Yvonne into the tribe. I attended and danced at her adoption ceremony the summer of 1984 at the Colony powwow. John Kauger is known as "Colony John" and is a modern-day John Seger.

The Kauger family of Colony opened and dedicated their Gallery of the Plains Indian in 1981 to the Cheyenne-Arapahoe tribe. Each year this gallery has an art show in conjunction with the powwow. Riverwoman and I are among the original Indian artists showing at this gallery since its opening. It is a privilege to have our pipes and pipebags on display at a historical site of the Cheyenne-Arapahoe people. Riverwoman is very much at home there because this is also near Cherokee country.

The Cheyenne-Arapahoe powwow in Colony usually begins Friday night with a peyote ceremony in a tipi. A peyote tipi is erected as well as a medicine tipi. Most folks attending the powwow set up camp at the grounds. The powwow grounds include a large clearing surrounded by forests of huge grandfather cottonwood trees. I often wonder about the sights these old cottonwoods have seen. To the south of the grounds are the old school buildings. The Kauger family is trying to get these buildings restored and preserved as a historical site.

In the four consecutive years I have attended this powwow, I have never seen anyone drunk or disorderly. There is no alcohol consumed there. It is a time of family reunion. The old ones are there. Cheyenne-Arapahoes gather from Montana, the Dakotas, Kansas, Wyoming, Nebraska, Colorado, Texas, and New Mexico. My warrior society brother, Sapa, half Cheyenne and half Swiss, flies in from Switzerland for this powwow. The spectators range from cowboys and their families to artists, professors, and judges from Oklahoma City, as well as neighboring Kiowa and Comanche Indians. All are welcome in peace and in comfortable hospitality. Of all American Indian powwows I've attended, the friendliest and most hospitable toward all people are the Cheyenne-Arapahoe.

I walk taller and prouder for months after attending one of my own tribal powwows. It is a powerful feeling to bring friends and neighbors to a large gathering of your people for the purpose of bragging about them, and to offer folks a warm, deep, unforgettable event. Such is a Cheyenne-Arapahoe powwow!

The Oklahoma summer days in late August are hot and humid. The nights are cool, comfortable, and breezy. The dancing at the powwow begins at sunset and continues till dawn. There are hundreds of dancers out there, sometimes with three sets of drummers and singers. The grand entrance of all the dancers led by the warrior society of Vietnam veterans gives one goose bumps. The women "buckskin dancers" look regal in their white hide dresses, fully beaded yokes, and full-length fringe. The old-time traditional "straight dancers" are awesome as they stalk their imagined prey with yellow and black painted faces. The "fancy dancers" twirl circularly with purple and yellow dyed feathers. The poker-faced, provocative "gourd dancers" are a testimony to the continuing prevalence of the traditional medicine of the peyote religion.

The smell of Indian frybread tacos and buffalo meat abounds and permeates the cool Oklahoma summer night breeze. There are many food stands. No one—spectator, visitor, or participant—leaves a Cheyenne-Arapahoe powwow hungry. You hear the sound of the drums below you, as if coming out of the earth, the sound of the breeze in the cottonwood leaves above you, and in between the high-pitched wailing of women singing coming straight at you. It makes you smile and feel glad to be alive. You look around and hear an inner voice singing, "The Cheyenne-Arapahoe are strong and still alive. They dance. They sing. They live. A-ho."

During the hot, humid days of the powwow, warrior societies meet. There are giveaways, and relatives visit and socialize under the shade of the tall cottonwoods. During such afternoons I have received advice and teaching from Chief Archie Blackowl while sitting with him, his wife and sons, and my society brother, Sapa. Sapa became Archie's son and I became his brother, for over the years, Sapa helped him with the sun dance at Concho, Oklahoma, while I made some traditional pipes for use in the sun dance and for certain medicine bundles. In exchange, Archie instructs us in "the proper way to go" regarding the Cheyenne religion. Sapa and I are highly honored to have been accepted as family by Archie Blackowl, one of the head chiefs of the southern Cheyenne, and also a peyote man.

One afternoon, I was complaining to Archie that an Indian pipemaker from another tribe was openly criticizing my pipes, insinuating that my artwork lacked authentic traditional design. I was unhappy because I sensed ego and jealousy instead of unity and support among some Indian artists creating sacred pipe designs. Archie told me, "Don't worry, when you're good, they notice ya'. But when they start talkin' about ya', that means you're damn good---ha-ha-ha-ha." We laughed on and off all afternoon about this. To this day, any time anyone offers the slightest criticism of my art designs, I begin laughing as I recall Archie's words.

One of my most memorable and sacred experiences with Archie Blackowl was during a new moon in autumn when I visited him at his home. I delivered a "straight pipe" to him for a priest's bundle. He performed a paint ceremony on me, using the sacred red Cheyenne paint from Bear Butte. He also gave me some paint and showed me how to perform this ceremony for members of my warrior society.

Our warrior society is called "the Redtail Hawk Medicine Society." In New Mexico, it is known as "the Redtail Hawk Medicine Society." It was organized by Nantan Lupan and James Bluewolf as a result of a strong vision given to Nantan Lupan by the redtail hawk. The society was founded in 1974 and fulfills Hopi prophecy that new clans and societies shall

emerge as part of a larger revival and purification of
the Red Road. The society is indicative of the pan-
American Indian unity movement in that it is an intertribal society.

The center of the society is the sacred pipe. I am
currently blessed with the privilege of being the pipeholder of the society pipe. I am also pipeholder and
spokesman for the society in New Mexico. Originally,
this began as a society of dog-soldier brothers during
the Alcatraz and Wounded Knee days. Today it has
evolved into a warrior (caretaker) and medicine society
of service to elders of all tribes. Its activities include
teaching, counseling, community service, and the revival and perpetuation of traditional Indian medicine
for religious purposes and as tools of self-realization.

The society initiated its first woman warrior member
(Riverwoman) after a sun dance in 1982. Society members travel to churches, schools, and drug-rehabilita-
tion clinics as consultants and lecturers. Last year, I
gave a weekend seminar at the University of California in Los Angeles on the sacred pipe and the Medicine Wheel. Society members have served as helpers
in medicine camps such as Rolling Thunder's in
Nevada and Grandfather Csamu's in California.

Chief Archie Blackowl is proud of the medicine of
the Redtail Hawk Society. He, like other chiefs, is
aware that more and more people are going out alone
or in small private groups to perform ceremonies such
as the sun dance. Many are taking up the old way to
strengthen themselves for the people and to strengthen
the Red Road Indian way.

During the years 1980 through 1983, I witnessed
an oil boom in Western and Southern Oklahoma as
I attended the Cheyenne-Arapahoe powwow in Colony each summer. I also traveled regularly to Arapahoe, Oklahoma, to quarry alabaster and marble. (Ted

Creeping-bear, a Kiowa sculptor, and I were the first artists to introduce Oklahoma marble and alabaster to the New Mexico art scene. We were the trailblazers for interest in this carving stone among Santa Fe stone carvers.) During this time, there was discovered in Oklahoma what is known as "The Anadarko Basin," an underground natural gas formation beginning at Weatherford and extending in a zigzag pattern down through Colony and through parts of Kiowa and Comanche country to Anadarko, a distance (as the crow flies) of about 90 miles. This gas formation zigzagged its way through the heart of Cheyenne-Arapahoe and Kiowa-Comanche country. You could trace its course at night by the blinking red lights of the gas-drilling rigs.

If your property happened to be in the path of its pattern, you would probably get a drilling rig on your property, with a monthly lease payment of perhaps $7,000! And most of these drilling rigs were being leased on Indian land. Some families had two and three rigs on their property. Small-town businesses in Colony and Weatherford were booming with activity.

The natural gas people seemed fair and honorable, with a respect and consideration for the environment. I socialized with them in restaurants and motels and also visited their drilling sites, which were landscaped and well kept. The Indians, Anglo farmers, and local businesses were all making money. Everyone was happy. I don't understand the economics of it all, but the price of gasoline was slightly decreasing during this boom in Oklahoma. It was a classic example of how such things could be accomplished peacefully among people and in harmony with nature.

More significantly, during those years I watched the Cheyenne-Arapahoe, Kiowa, and Comanche tribes use the money they received from this natural gas boom (both individually as families and collectively as a tribe) in wise and commendable ways. They improved their personal standard of living, revived tribal traditions and ceremonies, took more control of their respective Indian centers, and poured money into education and the development of their tribal art. During those years, there began a revival of Indian art in Oklahoma among Indians as well as Anglos. Indian artists were creating, and Anglo farmers, ranchers, and collectors were buying. It was a fine testimony of how things can be. The story is not all "peaches and roses," however, because the boom came to a sudden halt around 1984, and many folks suffered—from individual families to banks in Oklahoma City.

After the smoke cleared and the dust settled, the religion and art among many tribes in Oklahoma had been given a boost in upward growth and momentum that continues today. As for me personally, I learned much about my medicine through contact with my southern Cheyenne-Arapahoe relatives in Oklahoma. I will always be proud of the way most Cheyennes and Arapahoes managed their money from that Anadarko Basin natural gas boom of the early 80s. And when I recall the powwow days in Colony among my Cheyenne-Arapahoe people, I can hear the southern breeze rustle the cottonwood leaves, and the high-pitched wailing of the Cheyenne-Arapahoe women singers. The spirits of long-ago Cheyenne and Arapahoe warriors and chiefs—such as Left Hand, White Crow, Little Raven, Yellow Bear, Little Robe, Red Moon, Black Kettle, Stone Calf, White Shield, and Bull Bear—still gather in council at the old Indian school grounds in Colony, bearing witness and silent affirmation to the continuing gatherings and celebration of their twentieth-century descendants, and I among them.

12
Sorcery or Medicine?

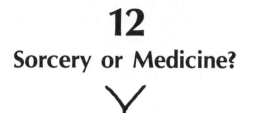

From time to time I am approached by some people "seeking power." They seek me out and request to learn from me. I advise them that I will go alone and fast and pray, to seek guidance about them. They should do the same about me. If and when appropriate, they will learn with me, through me. I ask some what they want to learn. They reply they want power. My concern is, power for what? Do they want to control a lover, make money using power, influence political decisions? Do they want to change their behavior, remove a negative attitude within themselves? There is war medicine, healing medicine, weather medicine, power to summon the wind or lightning, power of nature's elements while on a quest, etc. The purpose of medicine is inner balance and outer harmony, from which comes power, medicine power. It is appropriate and natural to use one's medicine power to obtain goals, work on projects, or to combat personal struggles in survival. But use of one's power must be in a sacred manner, with compassion for other beings. To use personal spiritual power to manipulate a person, object, or situation, is dangerous and not pure. Even the Ultimate Reality, the Creator and Source of existence, does not manipulate creation against its will. We are created with a free will, even to cause our own suffering.

When the primary and almost exclusive purpose of seeking and of making medicine is solely for power, when power becomes the priority above and beyond all else, at that point a person enters into the realm of sorcery. Sorcery is not always negative, but it is dangerous. How power is used deems it negative or positive, destructive or constructive. A sorcerer is interested in gaining and protecting personal power. Some sorcerers challenge one another in power confrontations. A medicine person (man or woman) is interested in developing and maintaining personal balance, collective harmony, and communion with the Great Spirit. A person of power may not be actively seeking to be of the Great Spirit; power is not used by all people to edify creation or to glorify the Great Spirit. I have attended some gatherings where people of power are jealous and feel threatened by one another. My choice is to confront such pettiness or to leave. Usually I leave. I do not channel any energy in their direction. I would rather visit a hospital and channel energy toward a cancer patient. However, most gatherings I have attended are comprised of medicine people ready to share and to exchange energy and feelings, to unify power to offset war, disease, and destructive influences.

All power originates from the Great Power, the Great Spirit. This power is individualized in unique energy packets the physicists call "quanta." These energy packets are particles and waves, usually both, as light consists of particles and waves. On a larger level, the power of God the Great Spirit is individually manifested as energy combinations forming plant, animal, mineral, and human. All manifestations are interconnected. The energy of creation is intrinsically positive, striving for order, harmony, and balance. The earth purifies itself regularly in cycles over millions of years, as evidenced by glaciers, floods, earthquakes, and volcanoes. All this activity of the energy of God manifesting and maintaining its pure positive energy is medicine, medicine of the Great Medicine.

To define, classify, or categorize any individual or collective energy of creation as intrinsically evil is negative sorcery; it abuses energy. Atomic energy is a wondrous thing and a powerful expression of creation. The atomic bomb is an awesome destructive harness of this energy. Certain animals, plants, or rocks may be chosen by the spiritual world to convey a specific message, as on a vision quest. Some animals, plants, or rocks are chosen as carriers of certain types of messages. The owl, for example, often but not exclusively, brings unpleasant messages to humans from the Great Spirit. These messages may be of sickness or death. A sorcerer may caution someone about the bad omen of the owl, the snake, or the black widow spider. These animals don't seek out humans to attack or terrorize. They go about their business of survival. But we emotionally and fearfully identify the message with the messenger. If I tell you about a flat tire on your car, do you accuse me of flattening your tire?

Years ago while teaching and counseling on the Pit River Reservation in northern California, I was driving a medicine woman to an Indian center. During our conversation about the medicine of the owl, a huge horned owl soared across the highway in front of my truck. We both giggled nervously and wondered if the owl's message that day was for us. When we arrived at the Indian center, I was told that Riverwoman had been trying to contact me all day. My message was to call the hospital. I finally discovered that my infant son, Trinity, had pneumonia but would be healed in time, without permanent harm. The Great Spirit was trying to contact me that day through the owl. But the owl did not bring the pneumonia to my infant son.

Often we assume the owl's message to always be unpleasant. It usually is, but not always. The medicine of the owl is also night vision and the gentle wisdom learned in sleep. When owls or crows are seen just before deaths or during funerals, the collective consciousness of a group or tribe of people over a period of time forms an exclusive association with that animal. We Cheyennes know the owl as "mistai," which is the same word we use for ghost. We get nervous and giggle when we see an owl, but we don't condemn it or judge its presence as a bad omen. Warning signs in nature may authentically occur, but bad omens are in people's thoughts, feelings, and behavior, and these too are human abuses of their positive pure power.

All creatures and critters are manifestations of the Divine. But don't expect all life forms to snuggle up next to you and cuddle. Some are poisonous. Some plants will heal you, some can kill you. Some animals will lick you, others will bite you. Some rocks and minerals can enlighten you, others can harm you. Some are more friendly than others. Some are not friendly at all, and there is usually a reason. The rattlesnake, for example, rarely smiles and would rather crawl away and hide or bite. The first reaction people have toward a rattlesnake is to kill it. The rattlesnake is not happy because of this. Also, today most animals that live inside the earth and beneath its surface feel the pain and abuses inflicted on Earth Mother and the environment, more so than other life forms. It is part of their duty to express the pain and displeasure of nature due to abuses and the persistent lack of compassion toward nature's sentient beings.

The gaining and development of energy focused and concentrated as power is guided by the code of the natural law of the universe. In all its uses and abuses, we are held accountable. For every action, there is a reaction, for every gain a loss, and for every loss there is a gain. Those whose thoughts, actions, and feelings support nature will flow with its rhythm. Those who abuse nature will cause conflict and experience struggle. This is the law of life and applies to all of us, regardless of our theology and dogma or doctrine. To gain power is to focus and to concentrate the energy within and around us. Our relationship with this power depends on how we use it. Our direction with this power may be the path of sorcery or the Medicine Road. To use energy to power ourselves in self-realization and God-communion, instead of power over another in manipulation, is good medicine.

13
Native Indian Healing

When I returned to Montana after completing school in Ohio and Michigan, I was proud to have become the first in my family to graduate from a college or university. But I was psychologically depressed, emotionally confused, and physically weak. Although it was exciting with never a dull moment, it was tough to be a college student in the 1960s. During those years, my closest friends were black people, and I became involved in their struggle for justice and social change. I witnessed the student murders by the National Guard at Kent State University in Ohio, marched on Washington, D.C., with Martin Luther King and Dr. Benjamin Spock, and was shot at by the Ku Klux Klan while organizing a voter registration in Georgia. My nerves were taxed and my body burdened from the abuse of amphetamine diet pills, which I naively used to regain classroom time lost due to my outside involvements (and also to prepare for tests). My college education substantially included out-of-classroom "field experience"!

When I arrived back in Montana, the Kennedy brothers and Dr. King were dead, several of my friends

114

and college roommates had died in Viet Nam or from drug overdoses, and I had grown disillusioned about how the medicine of Indian shamans and priests could effectively deal with all I had experienced and witnessed those years away at school in the East. I had become a cynic. My father looked into my eyes and said, "If this is what college does for you, I'm glad I was spared the experience!"

At that time, it was a wise and powerful thing my grandmother Medicine Rock did for me when she chose the vision quest as the ceremony to teach me. This was her response to my arrogant challenge that Indian ritual is merely a cultural pastime. No logical positivist or dialectical materialist could have had more skepticism or objectivity than I had when I climbed that mountain in the Valley of the Moon nineteen years ago. I acknowledged that faith might have power and value, but I discovered for myself that there is also the power of what is experienced, witnessed, and perceived. On a spiritual path, the acceptance and subsequent use of that which is seen (perceived) and that which is unseen (believed) can provide a harmonious tool of power for discernment.

Sharing with Spirit and Nature

On that vision quest I discovered two things: I discovered the Great Spirit and I discovered my Self. This was not the self of my ego; I was well in contact with that. I discovered the soul, spark of the Great Spirit in me. I began to realize the Great Spirit as the Source of life, the universal principle of order, the principle of principles, often called "the natural law of the universe." It is the matrix of stone and the grain in wood.

I now both perceive and believe that the Great Spirit is the power of the sun, and the power of the sun is in every atom of every created thing. All that is created and existing is alive with its own unique level of power and of intelligence. The power and intelligence of the Great Spirit, uniquely expressed and manifested in each created thing, is capable of being contacted and shared. It can be shared between humans, between humans and animals, as well as between plants, animals, and minerals. The elements as well—fire, earth, the winds, the waters—are capable of sharing their power and intelligence. All created things have an intelligence and possess a knowledge of the Great Spirit that is in them.

Spirit medicine drawing
of John's higher self

To share this knowledge of the Source a contact must be made and a relationship formed. If a stranger approaches you demanding something from you, you are apt not to respond. If that stranger introduces himself and acknowledges you by asking your name, a contact is made. In time, as more information and experiences are exchanged between you, the person is no longer a stranger. You feel safe and comfortable enough to progressively share information. Eventually a relationship may form.

This also applies to our contact with spirit and nature. If we approach the Great Spirit and nature as a demanding stranger, most often we will not receive a response, or perhaps we will elicit a frightening or unfavorable response. This is the basis for introducing yourself and bringing a tobacco offering to a cedar tree, for example, before gathering its leaves for use in ceremony. Introduce yourself to the cedar and tell it why you are gathering its leaves. Ask its permission. Perhaps sing it a song. Leave a gift or offering behind instead of coming only to take, as a predator. Embrace the cedar. Sit in silence beneath it and listen. Perhaps it will share some of its secrets of healing. Plants often prefer to communicate in the language of silence. In this sacred manner, one approaches nature to ask her to share her secrets as a relative. It is an experience in concentration and patience to form a medicine relationship with a plant being, and even more so with a rock or mineral being.

This contact and relationship directly with the Great Spirit, a spirit guide (the Great Spirit's messenger), the Great Spirit manifested in nature, or with the Great Spirit in you (the Self) is the purpose of the vision quest. It is also the foundation for the making of medicine, that is, discovering the knowledge of spirit in all created things. Such was the way the ancient elders and native visionaries acquired information. The ordeal of acquiring such knowledge of the divine in all things comes by holy communion with life. This yields a perennial peace and joy in spite of pain and negativity that continually comes and goes. This resulting peace and joy is as healing as the physical medicinal properties of plants and minerals and of the elements such as fire and water. This is the basis of native healing and Indian medicine, whether it be herbal healing or healing associated with ritual and ceremony. Ceremony and ritual, I discovered on that first vision quest, can be either a superstitious abuse or an intelligent use of the natural law to contact and form a relationship with the power of the Great Spirit.

Ever since my first vision quest, and even to this day, I have observed carefully how a medicine healer uses a feather or a talon to contact the Great Spirit to heal a sick person. I observe each style with the attention of an intern observing a surgeon performing an operation, for I have discovered over the years the healing authenticity of both ancient and modern approaches. The two techniques are a result of different levels of contact and relationship with the healing power of the Great Spirit.

For the next ten years after my first vision quest, I lived in villages and in the camps of men and women medicine teachers, both in my tribe and in other tribes. I traveled with them to many reservations as their student, assistant, and sometimes as their bodyguard. Each summer solstice I would go out on a vision quest from one to four days. My medicine teachers always cautioned me to practice what I preached and to preach only what I practiced. They also taught me the value and necessity of regularly renewing my vision and medicine power, that receiving vision and obtaining power was not enough, that I must continually keep my vision clean and my medicine pure, especially if chosen to become a healer or channel for people in need.

I see a growing number of people today performing and conducting healings. My hope is that they themselves strive for purification. My prayer is that I, as a teacher and a healer, continually strive for self-cleansing and purification, to be a clean channel for those folks whom the Great Spirit sends to me. I pray for the guidance and strength to practice what I speak and speak only that which I practice. May my talk be my walk, and my walk my talk.

When people have a clean spirit and their medicine power is strong from personal contact with God and close relationship with nature, their healing power is felt by merely being in their presence, before they speak a word or begin a ceremony. The power of their countenance precedes their words and behavior. They are known by the fruits of their being as well as by their words. Their presence becomes a substantial part of their healing power.

Treating Addicts

While traveling among different reservations with medicine teachers, a problem we regularly were requested to address was alcohol abuse and drug addiction. Spiritual practices such as the vision quest, sweat lodge, and pipe ceremony were effective therapeutic tools in dealing with alcohol and drug abuse. The experience of the actual ceremony was healing, but equally powerful were the tasks and activities necessary for the preparation required before participating in these ceremonies. Before touching the sacred pipe in a pipe ceremony, for example, an individual could not be drunk or "stoned" from a drug. Participating in a sweat ceremony requires fasting for a day, and we have to guard our thoughts around the sweat lodge. A vision quest requires being alone in nature from one to four days without food, sometimes without water. The vision quest often serves as a detoxification period for heavy drinkers. Sometimes those days out questing were a person's longest time sober in months or years. This was a beginning. A long journey of recovery has to begin with the first step.

The preparation for these ceremonies involves attention training, concentration through will power, and disciplined behavior. This is the basis of self-discipline, a voluntary discipline imposed freely by one-

self, the attaining of which exercises one's dynamic
will power. People ask to learn power and seek it. The
Great Spirit created us with will power. It is a gift to
be exercised. Self-discipline and will power are tools
of behavior change. Behavior change is the basic
building block for the recovery of an alcoholic or a
drug addict, or for any person with a problem. Establishing self-confidence by progressively successful
acts of will power is the beginning of the road to
recovery.

If a person says, "I'm an alcoholic and I'm miser-
able," in the sweat lodge you gently assert, "Change
your behavior from that of getting drunk to that of remaining sober." Such people ask how, and a dialogue
begins. They are there in the sweat lodge talking about
their behavior instead of in a bar drinking. Or perhaps
they are but on the side of a hill, away from their usual
environment of home, job, and gin mill, smoking a
prayer pipe and talking about life, taking a look at
themselves for the first time in years. This is the basis
and goal of what therapy attempts to achieve in con-
ventional psychology. If a spiritual manifestation occurs during ceremony, the excitement, well-being,
and joy become a bonus beyond the psychological experiences of well-being and self-confidence. The deep
and complete feeling of spiritual peace propels them
forward to want to go farther, to experience more. Fear
begins to dissolve. They feel good in spite of their ad-
dictive attempts to feel bad.

If you asked alcoholics or drug addicts if they want
to develop self-discipline, will power, and change
their behavior, most often they would laugh in your
face. But if you could challenge them to experiment
with something new, especially with the possibility
that they could prove it wrong, ineffectual, or useless
to their dilemma or situation, you may challenge them

and stir them to act, even when nothing seems to interest them but drink or drugs. My grandmother used the power of my arrogance to teach me a ceremony so that I could prove it ineffectual. In choosing the vision quest, she wisely provided me with a means by which my whole life's behavior would have a new focus. She was a good therapist.

Due to my extensive experiences in working with alcoholics and drug addicts traveling with different medicine teachers and healers, for ten years I was employed as a professional therapist in alcohol clinics and drug rehabilitation programs in Arizona, California, and New Mexico. My positions there provided me with professional training in psychology, physiology, and therapy. During those years I was also employed as a high school and college teacher and guidance counselor. My counseling positions eventually took me into the realm of marriage and vocational counseling. One of my most rewarding positions was as a career counselor at Albuquerque Technical Vocational Institute. Soon after that, I began my own private practice as therapist. Today my counseling services are primarily spiritual.

In all counseling, whether it be for alcohol or drug abuse or marriage or vocational problems, I have realized there is no substitute for authentic contact between therapist and client. If the counselor can form a real contact and develop a sharing relationship with the person in need, then a foundation is established between them upon which other things can develop. If that initial contact is missing, a relationship of sharing and exchange does not develop, and the therapist may as well lecture to a wall. The most sophisticated therapeutic techniques in psychology are as "water off a duck's back" to a client who is not listening. The social contact between client and therapist must be kept professionally objective and structured. Therapists do not have to become close friends with the clients they counsel.

Once a contact and relationship begin, both client and therapist can develop a plan for the client to do better, whether coping with problem behavior or spiritual seeking. At each session, the plan is evaluated by both client and therapist and either expanded or changed. This is the basis for developing a client's individual self-realization and awareness. The power of the client's own will, self-realization, and awareness can heal, spiritually enlighten, and change behavior. It is a process that requires development in time, but its initial movement creates a positive, healing momentum. The start is half the finish.

Spirit and Nature: Male and Female

The Great Spirit "outside" form is spirit. The Great Spirit manifested "in" form is nature. The universal principles of spirit and nature apply to all races, regardless of religion, political ideology, or philosophy. The same sun rises and sets on the black, red, white, and yellow people. The same moon waxes and wanes over the Hindu and the Christian. The four seasons of life are experienced by Asians and Caucasians. The style and form of peoples' contact and relationship with spirit and nature varies. Some groups and religions acknowledge spirit over nature, some nature over spirit. Approaches that favor either spirit or nature are inharmonious relationships with both and yield personal or collective disharmony. Some groups lose contact altogether with nature and spirit.

The division of life into categories of higher and lower, of spirit over nature, carries the dangerous implication of spirit as male, above lower nature as female. Spirit and nature, male and female, are uniquely different yet equal expressions and aspects of a common Source, the Great Spirit. To deny or to pass a lower judgment on either is to do so also to the male or female within each of us. In doing so, sons or daughters of earth and sky reduce themselves to arrogant, spoiled children favoring father over mother or mother over father. They then find themselves in an unbalanced situation where the Great Spirit becomes exclusively male. The meaning of "woman" is reduced to one of the sexes, whereas the meaning of "man" becomes humanity. Opposing spirit to nature and to sexuality is not spiritual realization, but rather the male or female ego opposing that which it cannot control. I have witnessed inharmony based on this misconception between husband and wife during marriage counseling, as well as when assisting people to handle fear of nature during preparation for their vision quest.

To deny either the male or female aspect of the Great Spirit within us or in nature is to deny either the sun or the moon. To elevate one over the other is to wish sun would shine day and night or to wish moon would shine night and day. This inaccurate perception occurs collectively in some religious groups where God is considered exclusively male. It also occurs in individuals whose male and female sides are in opposition instead of in harmony and balance with one another. Such internal disharmony carries over into male-female relationships. Such one-sided people forget that the Great Spirit uses male and female to create new life for procreation as well as in relationships.

The use of the sacred pipe used in ceremony is not only a tool of focusing but is invaluable in counseling people having problems with spirit and nature, male and female. The bowl of the pipe is female with its hole as an egg or womb; the hole is also called the center (Source) of the universe. The stem of the pipe is male and is also all that grows on the earth. Stem and bowl are each unique, and each has its own shape and energy. Each part is beautiful and whole unto itself, yet they form a fuller beauty when joined, stem into bowl, creating beauty and energy different from that before joining. Together the stem and bowl breathe smoke.

As the sacred pipe is passed in a circle during some therapy sessions, it becomes a focusing tool in which participants begin to realize that male and female, spirit and nature, are expressions and extensions of themselves and of one another, not opposing outside forces or elements they have to deal with. A man, for example, then sees himself, his wife, and his teenage son as different manifestations of the same circle. Or during her vision quest, a young Indian woman views a dark countryside as an aspect of God capable of bringing her vision and revelation, instead of threatening elements to be dealt with. The sacred pipe focuses one's attention to see all life as relatives, not in a belief system of some esoteric religion, but in a realized and tangible way. Such vision is practical enough to solve problems, resolve relationships, remove fear, and strengthen families.

Healing medicine power can be experienced through a medicine wheel, a flower, a feather, a medicine bundle, a song or a ceremony, or from the rising sun or full moon. The task is to discover this power, not by logical analysis, but by reflecting, contemplating without thinking, without letting your mind get in the way. The mind is important in healing, but it is limited. It is like using the healing waters of the lakes, rivers, and streams. Silent contemplation using the power of spirit, however, is like using the healing waters of the rains falling from the sky which embrace all the earth and supply all lakes, rivers, and streams. It is healing to be still and to behold attentively, and then to focus and direct that calmness which may have otherwise been scattered or dissipated. It is healing to behold and to be attentive to outer nature and to the spirit in oneself. There is much power in learning by watching as well as by following a technical diagram. One learns and develops by feel as well as by study. The key is to harmoniously balance thinking and reflecting, mind and spirit, spirit and nature, earth and sky, and to view them as different entrances to the same circle.

Healing through Ceremonies

In alcohol detoxification clinics, rehabilitation centers, and schools on and off Indian reservations, among Indians and non-Indians, I have witnessed and experienced the learning power and therapeutic value of ceremonies and ritualistic practices. Smoking of the sacred pipe, the vision quest, the sweat lodge, the sun dance, the moon ceremony, and the setting up of the Medicine Wheel are all effective tools. They help people to acquire personal self-realization, and develop objective awareness. They are useful in changing abusive behavior and in strengthening marital and family relationships. They are effective aids to mental concentration in learning difficult subjects in school. I have witnessed their use and application among people of all ages and ethnic backgrounds. These ceremonies and practices do not represent a "cure-all," but they do illustrate and bear testimony to a group of tools that work for people in need of solving problems and in search of spiritual truth.

I have seen a retired Anglo army captain find a new meaningful career by using the medicine wheel to view more clearly his anxiety from the four perspectives of the four directions. I have seen an alcoholic Indian man remain sober for years after performing a sun dance, and then go on to train to become a school teacher. I have seen inmates at the New Mexico State Penitentiary resolve differences among themselves and the prison guards using the sacred sweat lodge ceremony. I have seen the effect of the use of the pipe bundle and the sweat ceremony command the respect of a prison warden toward Indian medicine as authentic rehabilitation beyond mere cultural pastime. I have seen families identify problems with their children and steadily work together to resolve those problems, using the sacred Medicine Wheel as a vehicle for weekly family get-together, instead of dumping their problems onto social workers outside the family. I have seen an Anglo woman, a chronic drug addict for twenty years, turn her life around toward health and balance after a vision quest experience. She had been in several rehabilitation programs and was known as a "professional patient," in that no therapy had dented her drug abuse problem. I saw a group of problem teenagers in a residential group home in Sante Fe, New Mexico, begin to share openly problems and fears after sharing the sacred pipe in a circle. Previous to that pipe ceremony, all structured attempts at trying to open these children to sharing in group therapy had failed.

Those teenagers discovered a new relationship with a pipe—instead of dulling their senses, it sharpened them. I have seen countless business and professional people of all races and backgrounds, whose habitual straining of the mind was temporarily relaxed by the use of drugs and alcohol, discover a peace and a calm within themselves in silent contemplation in nature. In discovering a more natural means of calming their restlessness and frustration, using the sound of their own breath while in solitude, they learned to walk through life without "crutches." I saw an artist in Santa Fe gradually break his dependence on cocaine by sitting alone with the pipe and merely contemplating its meaning.

I know these people and have seen these things. By being of service to them in their needs and problems, I have learned more about the power and application of the ceremonies and practices of Native Indian healing and medicine. As John Fire Lame Deer continually reminds us, "These things are alive. They can take you where you want to go."

14

A Hopi Healer's Power

When my son Trinity was very young and began to walk his first steps, we noticed that he was having difficulty standing normally. He walked on the inside of his ankles with both feet bent outwards. For almost a year, we took him to different specialists in big cities and spent much money allowing each new specialist to try out his theory for foot braces. One specialist would prescribe shoes to point Trinity's feet inward as he walked, while another would prescribe a foot brace to point his feet outward. I was nearly hopeless as I watched his feet and walking get progressively worse in spite of all the specialists. It seemed as though they were experimenting in the dark; their diagnoses were contradictory to one another.

A Pima Indian friend in Phoenix, Arizona, asked me why, since I was Indian, I had not yet tried a medicine healer. I told him I was in the southwest far from home and was not acquainted with healers nearby. He suggested that I go to Hopiland in northern Arizona, and he offered to accompany us with Trinity. So within a week, we traveled to the village of Hotevilla on Third Mesa Hopiland. I was amazed to see the traditional Hopis living in dwellings at sites they had occupied for centuries. The village of old Oraibi is one of the oldest continuously inhabited villages on the North American continent.

We arrived in Hotevilla on a hot afternoon in August. My Pima friend took us to Grandfather David Monongyne's house. He is a village elder and one of the spiritual leaders of all traditional Hopis. His wife Nora went to get him as he was praying and smoking with other village elders in their kiva. As I sat on their porch waiting that summer afternoon, I felt removed from the rest of the world. I knew I was in a power spot. On the rooftop of the house across the road a Hopi man plucked two feathers from a live golden eagle, which had been tied by its foot to the roof. These "live" feathers would be used for dancing and healing.

From around the corner of the house came Grandfather David, guided by his carved walking stick, his wife, and another elder. I saw a short, aged man, grinning widely. He was wearing a red headband and with a blue blanket over his shoulder. I discovered later that he was almost completely blind and over a hundred years old.

We went inside his house and sat around a table. Nora served us some juice and frybread. I gave Grandfather David some cornmeal and a sack of potatoes, introduced myself, and told him my story and need concerning my young son. He leaned toward me and listened intently.

After I had finished speaking, Grandfather David asked me how old my son was, his name, and what kind of food he was eating. Then he asked me to bring Trinity to him. He sat Trinity on his lap and in Hopi language sang him a song about a cat. Then he began feeling Trinity's feet, ankles, and legs, carefully inspecting them by touch. Nora and the other Elder looked on carefully. Granfather David asked us to have Trinity walk back and forth across the room. As Trinity did so, Grandfather questioned Nora and the other elder. They both carefully verbalized their observations of Trinity's walking. After about twenty minutes, Grandfather asked us if we could remain for the night. We were surprised as we hadn't planned on being away overnight. But we decided that little Trinity's well-being had priority above everything, and Grandfather's invitation and hospitality were an honor. So we agreed. Grandfather was very pleased and said he would begin working with Trinity at sunrise the following morning.

We awoke about an hour before sunrise and had breakfast. At sunrise Grandfather went to the wood stove and sat on a small wooden stool. He emptied the ashes out of a small clay pipe, filled it with tobacco, and began to smoke. The room became quiet as he smoked his pipe. He held each puff of smoke in his mouth for a while, cocked his head upward, and slowly released the puff. The smoke expanded and floated upward, carrying his prayers to sky and beyond.

Then he asked me to bring Trinity close to him. He exhaled smoke over Trinity's legs and feet and more smoke over his arms and hands. He called out directions in Hopi to Nora. She began boiling water and putting herbs in it. When it was brewed, Grandfather directed her to pour this "tea" into a pan and set it on the floor next to him. He sang some Hopi songs, and he stuck his finger in the pan of water every fifteen minutes or so.

After a while, he directed me to put Trinity's feet in the pan of tea. Trinity soaked his feet in the warm tea for about ten minutes. Then Grandfather began

massaging Trinity's feet and lower legs in the tea.
After this, he sat Trinity on his lap and slowly rotated
each foot clockwise, then counter-clockwise. Rubbing
his own hands with the tea, he massaged it into Trinity's feet and lower legs. Grandfather David did this
slowly, carefully, and deliberately, with concentration, for about thirty minutes. Trinity was laughing
and giggling. He was in his grandfather's lap! Then
he had Trinity walk back and forth across the room
as he asked Nora questions, which she answered. Trinity walked almost completely normally! I got excited
and exclaimed, "He's healed." Grandfather said, "No,
not yet. But he will be."

The rest of the day we visited with Grandfather and
met the rest of his relatives. I asked him if he would
finish healing Trinity's feet. He told me that I should
heal Trinity because I was his parent. He instructed
me how to prepare the tea and how to massage and
rotate Trinity's ankles. He explained that this had to
be done twice every day, first thing in the morning,
last thing at night. He said it would take months, but
it would work. He also cautioned us not to think bad
thoughts as we massaged Trinity's feet and ankles.
As we left, I told Grandfather I would return soon and
asked if I could bring him something he needed. He
laughed and asked me to bring him some Kentucky
Fried Chicken.

For the next two moons (months), Riverwoman and
I took turns doctoring Trinity's feet every day as instructed. Every day, all day, Trinity was walking normally on his feet instead of leaning on his ankles as
he had been doing for the previous year. I felt much
affection and gratitude for Grandfather David and all
the Hopi people. I had spent so much money on med-
ical specialists and had experienced the heartache of
witnessing Trinity's foot abnormality grow worse

through it all. Now a little old man at a remote village in the desert not only performed the correct method of doctoring our son, but taught his parents how to do it themselves—for some cornmeal and a sack of potatoes!

Months later on a Friday afternoon, I loaded my truck with my sleeping bag and my pipe bag and medicine bundle. I told Riverwoman I was on my way to Hopiland to bring Grandfather David some Kentucky Fried Chicken. On my way I stopped and got two large buckets of chicken and two dozen ears of corn on the cob. I arrived at Grandfather's house in Hotevilla shortly after sunset. It was perfect timing. He and Nora and one of his grandsons, Harlon, were just about to prepare dinner. When I announced my presence to Grandfather and told him what I brought with me, he exclaimed in joy, "Connecticut Fried Chicken, ha-ha-ha!" I said, "No, Kentucky Fried Chicken." He said, "I know, Connecticut Fried Chicken, ha-ha-ha." In time, I became only too familiar with Grandfather's "Indian humor."

He sent out to the village for some friends; about four elders soon arrived with Harlon's wife and children. We all feasted on chicken, corn, frybread, mutton stew, and coffee, late into the night. Every once in a while, Grandfather or one of the elders would exclaim loudly: "Hurray, Connecticut Fried Chicken," and everyone would laugh.

About eleven o'clock that night, Nora went to bed, Harlon and his family went home to their house around the corner, and I found myself alone with Grandfather and four Hopi elders. They each wore sneakers, headbands knotted on the side of their heads, and they had their hair tied in the traditional Hopi knot. Most often, the Hopi men tie their hair with simple white cotton string. The Hopis also wrap their

prayer feathers with this same white string. In time,
I was to learn the power of Hopi humility and simplic-
ity. Most tribes I know of either thank the Great Spirit
for power over their enemies (the adversary), or give
thanks for enemies making them stronger. The Hopis
are the only ones I know who bless their enemies in
their prayers.

This late night I was alone with Grandfather David
and four tribal elders. The room was dark with only
one small lantern on the table. Light from the burning wood stove flickered and all our shadows danced
on the walls and ceiling. I felt like I was in a cave or
underground. Grandfather asked if I had enough to
eat and if I could stay the night. I thanked him for
teaching me how to heal my son. He told me that a
father and mother have power to heal their son. I then
asked if I could give him anything for teaching me.
The elder's all looked at one another and then at
Grandfather David.

Grandfather began to explain that there was a problem of alcohol and drug abuse among the teenagers
in the village. Many of the young people would hang
around outside at night in the dark, using drugs and
alcohol during ceremonies instead of going into the
kiva. The elders requested professional counseling
assistance from some clinics off their reservation. In
return they received proselytizing missionaries in all
villages, telling them their problems with their children were due to their pact with darkness in their
pagan ceremonies. Grandfather told me that they indeed needed help, but they wanted Hopi teenagers
to solve their problems and remain Hopi, become
stronger Hopis, not convert to another religion. I
agreed completely.

Grandfather and the elders had heard that my medicine was strong in working with alcoholics and drug

addicts. They had heard of me as an Indian from up north who was employed professionally at a guidance clinic in Flagstaff, and that this Indian was using Indian medicine in helping Indian and non-Indians with substance abuse problems. They had planned to travel to Flagstaff to seek me out. They would be willing to pay me for my counseling services for their teenagers in their village. Grandfather proclaimed that it was the will of the Great Spirit that brought my son to him for healing and that they did not need to seek me out in Flagstaff. The other elders verbalized agreement in Hopi, and I also agreed that it was the will of the Great Spirit.

Then there was silence among us. The fire from the wood stove flickered, and our shadows danced against the walls and ceiling. The elders looked at me, blinking their eyes like innocent children, awaiting my response. Grandfather leaned his head toward me, ready to listen carefully.

I began by addressing them with the word Qua-Á, which means "grandfather" in Hopi. I told them it was my experience and vision that Native American religion among all tribes had valuable tools to solve everyday problems, as well as ceremonies for spiritual communion. Our medicine tools have magic but are also a means of developing practical solutions to daily problems. Indian families of all tribes should start taking the eagle feathers down off their walls and off their altars and start using them to solve their marital problems and to strengthen their families. For example, medicine bundles and objects could help children get better grades in school and help them to develop self-discipline, concentration, and clear perception. We all have strong medicine on our altars; it is good to hold them in respect in ritual for spiritual communion and to revere them on altars in a sacred manner.

But now is the time to use them also as psychological and social tools to solve problems such as drug abuse, financial problems, and career decisions.

As I spoke these things, Grandfather and the elders periodically uttered agreement in Hopi; their affirmations became louder as I continued. I went on to tell them that many non-Indians were now successfully using Indian medicine to solve their addiction problems. I explained the use of the Plains Medicine Wheel as a tool for developing attention, concentration, awareness, and self-realization in behavior change, as well as the use of strong ritual in the vision quest. Grandfather and the elders became excited and were now uttering their affirmations loudly in unison. Grandfather expressed that such use of the medicine was the old way, that it was the original intent for the medicine to help solve life's problems here on earth, in addition to communicating with the spirit world. I told Grandfather David and the elders that it was time to take the medicine out of our pouches and use it. We all said that we Indian people need not always seek therapeutic help outside our own religion.

I agreed to spend time in Hotevilla and be of service as a counselor to Hopi teenagers. Grandfather offered me pay for doing this. I explained that he had already healed my son, and in exchange for my services I would like to learn about the Hopi way while I was among them. They agreed to this. They were pleased with my offer of such an exchange of services between us.

For the next two years, I spent a weekend a month during the winter in Hotevilla and sometimes a week at a time during summer and autumn. I would stay at Grandfather's house or camp out in the desert. Sometimes I would haul up a few of my horses and ride my Appaloosa stallion, Spotted Feather, through the village. A trail of Hopi children would follow me, like a Pied Piper. My horses were important in working with the Hopi teenagers. No one could ride unless he or she was "straight" (not high on drugs or alcohol).

During these two years, I traveled with Grandfather David to gatherings and meetings throughout the Southwest. The Hopis and Navahos were, and still are, having problems with corporate developers desecrating natural sacred shrines (such as the San Francisco Peaks in Flagstaff, Arizona; Mount Taylor near Grants, New Mexico; and Big Mountain near Black Mesa). I attended several open hearings sponsored by the U.S. Forest Service where the wishes of the people were supposed to be heard. In sadness and outrage, I watched Forest Service officials and corporate developers patronize Grandfather David and the elders as senile old people. I witnessed some of the strongest confrontation against this disrespect coming from such Navajo clan mothers as Mrs. Whitesinger. I discovered that the "Indian Freedom of Religion Act" had no teeth but was only fancy words on paper.

Although my function in these matters was only as escort and protector of Grandfather David and some elders of one Hopi village, I was given permission to speak at a few gatherings such as the one at Mount Taylor. I wrote several newspaper editorials regarding the expansion of the ski resort in the sacred San Francisco Peaks. These peaks are very special for many reasons, on many levels. They are the shrine of the Hopi Kachinas. Mount Elden, a foothill of the peaks, is laden with sacred Navajo shrines and caves. Hopis, Navajos, and Indians from many tribes throughout America go there to fast and to pray. The site is a natural cathedral. However, it is prevalent in Anglo consciousness that if a site is not marked or if a man-made structure is not built on it, then the area is not considered a place of worship.

The area is also sensitive ecologically. These peaks contain a species of wildflower found to exist nowhere else on earth. The area is the only arctic zone in Arizona.

Most Hopis and Navajos originally agreed to let people go into a designated area to ski and to commune with nature in the original ski resort. They agreed about twenty-five years ago to respect these sacred peaks, to let people ski peacefully, and not to expand. But now a wealthy Mormon developer had come up with a plan to expand the ski resort, to clear a hundred-acre parking lot, to build a lodge and a bar, and to widen the road leading up to the resort from two lanes to four lanes. During debate on this heated issue, the Hopi villages were flooded with Mormon missionaries trying to convert the people. A number of Hopis converted; the Hopi Tribal chairman became a Mormon. It was no coincidence that once Hopis became Mormons the San Francisco Peaks were no longer a sacred shrine to them, and they voted for expansion and development of the ski resort.

This issue was not between Indians and non-Indians. There were many local people of all ethnic backgrounds who were appalled at the proposed development. Many locals, such as Melissa Jean Flick, whose forefathers were among the original settlers who lived in peace with the Indians for over a hundred years, fought desperately to have the peaks classified as a wilderness area. The controversy became so heated, complicated, and political that the original spiritual issue became overshadowed. The final decision was therefore handed over to officials in Washington, D.C. In a short time, Secretary of the Interior James Watts approved development and expansion of the ski resort in the San Francisco Peaks, betraying the original agreement with the Indians and blatantly ignoring all religious claims and the outcries of all the traditional Hopis and Navajos in Arizona and New Mexico. To this day, I can't hear the name of James Watts without a flood of sad memories.

Not all my experiences with Grandfather David and the Hopis were controversial or sad. One of the most moving moments I have ever witnessed was a meeting between a Tibetan Rimpoche and the Hopi elders in a kiva in Hotevilla. It was the fulfillment of both Tibetan and Hopi prophecies. I was blessed with the opportunity of sharing a private sunrise pipe ceremony with this Rimpoche.

Traveling the Southwest with Grandfather David Monongyne of the Sand Clan was like being in the presence of a Hopi Mahatma Gandhi. His medicine power was as the power of flowing water. His humor made everyone laugh from the pit of the stomach, even his adversaries. The magic of his medicine, whether on the road, in the market place, or in the kiva, was often nearly miraculous. I will always be grateful that my son walks normally. Grandfather David is truly a holy man. Learning about the Hopi way from him and among the Hopis has touched my heart and deepened my spirit forever.

15

A Woman's Prayer— A Brother's Dream

As I mentioned previously, Riverwoman Freesoul is my best friend and a sister in our warrior society. She was the first woman initiated into the Redtail Hawk Medicine Society. She was my wife from 1973 to 1982. Riverwoman is the mother of our eleven-year-old son, Trinity Swiftotter Freesoul, and has the spiritual role of "sacred woman" in three of my sun dances, which binds us together, forever, as spiritual brother and sister. Our relationship has changed over the years, but it will never end. Together we remain as parents and share this blessed and sacred responsibility in raising a young son of earth and sky.

Riverwoman is a pipe carrier. For awhile she counseled the female inmates at the New Mexico State Penitentiary. She helped them develop their pipe bundles. To my knowledge, River is the only Native American woman carving ceremonial pipes. We have been displaying our artwork together for fifteen years. She has won many awards.

River is a quiet, unassuming person. Her behavior speaks. She lives the Medicine Road instead of talking about it. This is why I'm telling part of her story, which is part of her dream.

John and Riverwoman Freesoul

When River and I were first married, she was totally committed to being a wife and friend to her new
husband. One winter evening while we were sitting
around the stove in our cabin in Montana, River overheard me tell some warrior society brothers that it had
been my wish since a very young boy one day to have
a son. The brothers shared their strong feelings of support and agreement about the strong medicine of having a son. River listened and remained quiet. When
our visitors left that evening, River seemed sad. I asked
her to share her feelings. She expressed that she was
sad over not being able to have children due to an
operation she had before she met me. I comforted her
by expressing that I had been aware of this fact before I married her. Furthermore, I had been just talking about past wishful thinking that night. So we
retired, but her heart was sad.

The next morning at breakfast River was excited,
with a bright gleam in her eye. She told me about her
dream the night before. She saw a young boy about
eight years old standing next to me in a pine forest.
We both wore plaid shirts, and the young boy was the
image of me. He was my son. River told me that winter
morning in Seeley Lake, Montana, that we were going to have a son. I laughed and assured her that it
could not happen because of her previous operation.
I also assured her that it was OK, that I did not feel
incomplete about her or our marriage. River was excited nonetheless and told me that nothing was im-
possible with the Great Spirit. I smiled and went about
my daily chores.

The following days River proceeded to tell our
friends and relatives that, although she was not then
pregnant, one day she and I would have a son and
he would look just like his father. Folks asked how
this could be. River told them the Great Spirit had re-

vealed it to her in a dream, that she prayed for a son
and the dream came that same night. Most folks just
smiled condescendingly but did not share in her excitement.

I cautioned River to stop telling folks so affirmative-
ly that we were, in fact, going to have a son. She continued to share her prayer and dream. I eventually
became embarrassed and grew irritated with her. So
I firmly requested that she keep her "wishful thinking" to herself. She stopped talking about it but continued to pray. Regularly she would go into the woods
alone with her prayer pipe.

My relatives and society brothers began to caution
me about "River's problem." They told me she was
misusing the medicine by trying to have the Great
Spirit grant her a son, when she herself had prevented
any such possibility by her own action as a young girl.
They also told me that she was having neurotic feelings of inadequacy as a new wife not being able to
fulfill her new husband's wish for a son.

I became progressively aggravated with the situation and toward Riverwoman. I had many discussions
with her. I told her the Great Spirit could not take back
her action of preventing children. Sometimes I was
harsh with her about this. We were looked up to by
our people, and her psychological preoccupation with
giving birth to a son was becoming bizarre to me.

River would sit and listen quietly, saying nothing.
She ceased openly expressing herself about the matter, but from time to time I would see her walking off
by herself toward the woods. I knew she was still making medicine for a child. One time in a society council meeting, I was formally requested once and for all
to clear the matter with River. I politely yet firmly
asked the council to back off. They did. And I backed
off from Riverwoman. Over the next year, River prayed
about it silently and privately.

The following year Wounded Knee was over. The elders advised us all in the American Indian movement that the time for violently fighting the government was over. Now was the time of medicine power, the need for spiritual tools. Strengthen and purify ourselves, they told us, and we strengthen our families. "Go home and make medicine," they requested. Since that time, there has been a revival in Native American spirituality and unity among all tribes.

After that River and I and most of our society and clan relatives went to the foothills of the Sierra Nevada Mountains in northern California, where I became employed as a teacher and guidance counselor at a local college and high school. It was there I learned silversmithing, and I sold jewelry, as well as stone sculpture, to the local townspeople. That same year (1974) I worked for Lee Marvin, who is a creative artist in his acting. We presented him with a pipe just before I quit working for him. Lee Marvin is a fine person and I wish him well. I saw him in Santa Fe ten years later in 1984. Our meeting was brief yet complete. He is an artist at what he does. Lee is always welcome at our home.

My clan brother Robert Swiftotter, a Kiowa pipe carrier, came to live with River and me. Our clan, as is our warrior society, is intertribal, one of the changes in tradition as a result of the Indian unity movement of the 1960s. His nickname was "Kiowa." He was a powerful pipe man and instructor of the medicine way of the Red Road. He performed a pipe ceremony atop a mountain during our marriage ritual. A rainbow formed above us during the ceremony. Kiowa was psychic. He was a visionary, as I discovered by living with him. Kiowa, River, and I were in "hog's heaven" at this time in northern California. Our activist days seemed over, money was coming in, and there were plenty of catfish and trout in those lakes and streams in California on the Oregon border. We went fishing three days a week and on weekends.

One early summer morning, Kiowa came rushing into the living room and proceeded to tell River and me about his dream the night before. We usually verbalized or recorded meaningful dreams in a journal first thing upon awakening. Kiowa was particularly excited about this dream. He told us that in his dream, he, White Eagle (my younger brother), and I went for a drive in his car. We drove deep in the woods to the end of a dirt road, where there was a huge white buffalo standing broadside in the road, turning its head, looking at us. Then Kiowa got out of his car, threw his car keys at me, and ran away with the white buffalo over a hill, leaving White Eagle and me alone in his car.

Kiowa was laughing hard at this account of his dream. He asked me if I knew what it meant. I told him that it was meaningful when anyone dreamt about a white buffalo, but that it was particularly significant when an Indian dreamt about a white buffalo. I advised him to smoke his pipe and reflect on this dream.

Riverwoman then proceeded to share her dream with Kiowa about having a son, our son. This was the first time in months she had spoken of it. Kiowa was attentive and supportive. He asked her to pray and reflect about her dream. River said she had been doing so. I asked Kiowa why he was encouraging Riverwoman about her dream. He asked me why I just finished advising him to pray and reflect about his dream. He then told River and me that the dream world was beyond logic and reason, that often we are instructed by the powers during sleep because our bodies are not as restless and our thinking minds don't interfere with our intuitive wisdom so much. River received support from Kiowa that early summer morning, as they shared their dreams over trout, eggs, and coffee.

The next morning Kiowa came dashing into the living room, gasping in excitement. But he talked slowly and deliberately as he related another dream he just experienced. He told River and me that in this dream he was in a dark room. He couldn't see anything, not even his own body. He heard a baby's cry coming progressively closer. Then the dream faded and ended. Kiowa then exclaimed to River, "You are going to have a baby, either a son or twins!" I said, "No, no." River said, "Yes, I knew it." Kiowa told River, "This is why you have been so irregular with your moon cycle. This is why you missed your moon this month!" I retorted, "No, no. Why are you planting this in her mind?" I stormed out of the house and left for the rest of the day. Kiowa was shouting as I left, "It's my dream, a dream from the Great Spirit."

When I returned that evening, Kiowa and I were both more relaxed, and we talked. I explained to him my concern for River's mental health and told him how preoccupied she had been in Montana about having a son. He said he understood and empathized with me. He said that he would never encourage anything to harm his favorite sister, River. At the same time, he related, he must deliver the messages of the Great Spirit. I told him it was my feeling that he was misinterpreting the message this time. We couldn't agree, so we stopped talking about it. We decided to hike to the top of Mount Lassen the coming full moon, to be alone together on a mountain and smoke our pipes as brothers.

The following week River and I decided that she should see a doctor about her menstrual irregularity, especially since her moon was now late almost a month. She went to several different doctors, each giving her a different opinion. We grew very concerned about possible disease in her female organs. All the while Kiowa remained silent, just looking on, smiling.

River decided it would be best for her to fly back home to see the specialist who was her doctor years ago, the doctor who had operated on her. I agreed. I was very concerned. Kiowa kept assuring me privately that River was a healthy pregnant woman. I just ignored him. So River took a plane home and saw the specialist. A day later she phoned to say the specialist wanted to do a pregnancy test, that there was one chance in 900 that she could get pregnant, based on the type of operation he had performed on her years ago. These past years River had thought that there was no chance at all of a pregnancy. Her doctor asked if she was going to sue him if she was pregnant. River told him that she was indeed pregnant and that she blessed him.

The day River arrived back in northern California, Kiowa and I drove her to a clinic for a pregnancy test. The following day we found out that she was indeed pregnant. I was sitting outside on a tree stump, feeling like the world's biggest fool, happy, though stunned. River and Kiowa were inside the house rejoicing and praising God. I told Kiowa he was going to be the godfather. He ran downtown telling everyone River was pregnant and that he was going to be a godfather of twins or a son. The rest of the day friends and neighbors came over to congratulate us. Our clan and society relatives, especially those with us in Montana like Daniel Wolf Bear, were shocked and embarrassed. This all happened a few days before the full moon.

That night we had a surprise visit. White Eagle and his brother Puma arrived from down south. We hadn't

seen or heard from them for almost a year. White Eagle
had just bought a Bronco jeep and wanted to put some
miles on it, so he decided to take a trip. Puma, who
never traveled, decided spontaneously at the last
minute to go along. Puma said he didn't understand
why, but he felt this was a medicine trip for him.

There was much rejoicing and excitement at this
surprise visit and at the news of River's pregnancy.
A fire was made outside and the pipe was passed in
a circle. The moon would be full in a day or two. We
all decided to travel to Greywolf's camp at French
Gulch, where there would be a gathering and a sweat
lodge ceremony for the full moon. Greywolf hadn't
seen White Eagle and Puma for years, and we could
tell many of our friends and relatives about River's
pregnancy.

A day later, on the morning of the full moon, we
packed Kiowa's car and White Eagle's jeep for the
three-hour trip. Kiowa was indignant when he discovered that I had planned to have River ride with him
in his car, and I would ride with White Eagle and
Puma in the new jeep to talk and visit with them during the three-hour ride. Kiowa practically demanded
that I drive his car and travel in it with River. From
now on, he said, I had to remain even closer to River,
since she was pregnant, and that was the way he said
it was going to be! I was to take his pipe and my wife
in his car. That was all we needed. We would be safe
and protected. I agreed because he was so firm about
it. Eagle and Puma kept asking me to ride with them
and made a comfortable seat for me in the rear. But
I declined. Kiowa sat in the rear seat they had prepared for me.

River and I left ahead of the others. They were going to stop in town for some groceries for the gathering. We arrived at Greywolf's near sunset. I told

everyone at the gathering we had a big surprise for them en route following us. No one had any idea White Eagle or Puma brother were in town. Folks kept asking where Kiowa was and why we came in his car without him. At about 11 o'clock that night, we were all retiring in preparation for an early sweat ceremony the following morning. I was disappointed. I thought Eagle, Puma, and Kiowa had stopped off somewhere to socialize at a restaurant. As I fell asleep, I thought, "Those guys are inconsiderate. Oh well, perhaps they will surprise everyone with a late night arrival."

About three in the morning I was awakened from a deep sleep by a woman named Mourning Dove. She told me White Eagle wanted to see me. I looked down from the loft where I slept, and White Eagle and some other folks were seated around a circular table with a lantern in the middle. There was utter silence. I climbed down the ladder. I asked White Eagle what took him so long to arrive. He didn't answer. He was staring into the kerosene lantern in the middle of the table. Nantan Lupan told me White Eagle would not speak until they had awakened me.

I asked Eagle where Puma and Kiowa were and what had taken them so long. Still staring at the lantern, Eagle said, "There was an accident." Was anyone hurt? Yes, Puma was in the hospital. Was Kiowa hurt? White Eagle now looked up from the lantern, his eyes gazing into mine. "Kiowa is dead," he said. Without thinking, I asked, "How do you know?" Eagle said, "He died in my arms." Was he kidding? Was this a joke? Where was Kiowa? White Eagle rose to his feet and said in a forced manner, "In all the years you have known me, have you ever known me to joke about death?"

Eagle then extended his hand toward me, turned his palm downward, and opened his clenched fist.

Kiowa's medicine bag dropped onto the table. Kiowa wore it tied around his neck in a knot, and he never took it off, not even when bathing. The string of his medicine bag had been cut. Kiowa was dead!

Nantan Lupan and some others blackened their faces with coal ash from the stove and went outside singing death songs. The dogs started howling. Women were crying. I turned away, climbed back into the loft, and lay awake next to Riverwoman. I was stunned in disbelief, not feeling anything, not believing it had happened. Riverwoman was awake, but she never spoke a word nor made a sound; she just stared at the ceiling.

As the sun rose the following morning, the reality and pain of it all sank deep into my chest. There was no sweat ceremony. My surprise news of what was coming en route behind us was of death—the passing over of Kiowa.

River, Eagle, and I left that morning. We visited Puma in the hospital. He had a gash in his hip and would require an operation and hospital care for a month. White Eagle had a sprained hand. Kiowa had died of massive head injuries. He was thrown from the jeep. Eagle and Puma were sitting in the front. Kiowa was sitting in the rear, where I had planned to be. White Eagle swerved to avoid hitting a deer crossing the road. The jeep skidded and then went into a roll. Even though he escaped serious injury, as the driver White Eagle was in deep pain and grief.

I asked White Eagle to show me the exact spot where Kiowa died. He agreed to take River and me there. At this spot was a patch of dried blood beneath a pine tree. Kiowa was always telling people that to be an Indian was to hug a tree. Buried partially in the dirt was his favorite bracelet that he wore everyday. I had given it to him years earlier as a gift. I lifted the bracelet out of the earth. Eagle was really surprised. He and the highway patrol had combed the area the day before, looking for possessions scattered from the jeep.

I looked up and discovered that we were at the base of Mount Lassen, the mountain Kiowa and I had planned to climb that full moon. It was the full moon now. Kiowa was dead, his spirit returned to Source. His spirit left his body at the foot of Mount Lassen, beneath a pine tree, next to a creek, during the full moon. I told White Eagle about Kiowa's dream of the crying child in the dark room. Kiowa passed over a day after we discovered River was pregnant. The new child was announced; Kiowa had departed.

The following day White Eagle, River, and I called a council meeting with our friends and relatives and offered the sacred pipe. We told everyone about River's prayer for a son, about Kiowa's dream of his own death and of his dream about River's son (or twins). I also told the council of how Kiowa made me ride in his car with Riverwoman, while he sat in the seat intended for me in the jeep. We buried Kiowa's pipe on top of a volcano.

Today, twelve years later, River and I have a twelve-year-old son. His name is Trinity Swiftotter Freesoul. He is named after his godfather Swiftotter, whom we affectionately knew as Kiowa. People are amazed at how much Trinity looks like me. But the older he gets, the more he looks like his mother. Our friends and relatives remind Trinity that he was prayed for, that he was the result of a woman's prayer and a brother's dream. We are saving Kiowa's bracelet for Trinity when he completes his vision quest.

For years after this happened, women who wanted to get pregnant and women who were already preg-

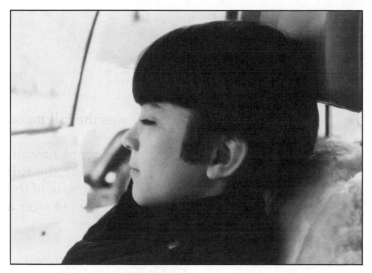

Trinity Swiftotter Freesoul—"dream child"

nant traveled to visit Riverwoman because her medicine is strong. Not too many folks nowadays criticize anyone's prayer or question a person's dream, as I had done. As for me, well, I decided to tell this story because River is quiet and doesn't talk about it much.

16
The Jesus Road

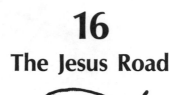

One winter years ago, my teacher at the time, Grey-wolf, asked me to go back home to Montana to check on some mutual friends of ours. James Buffalo Sun and Lila Full Night had gone to Montana near the Canadian border to hunt and prepare jerky. I had lived with Buffalo Sun for a while the previous year and he became like a brother. He was born and raised in the mountains and was the best hunter, tanner, tracker, and trail-blazer I ever met. We lived together in his hide tipi; he boasted he'd never live in a square house. Now he was up in northwestern Montana with eight-month-long winters and temperatures dropping forty below zero. So I thought I'd go up and tease him about living in a square log cabin.

Buffalo Sun was antisocial, a twenty-five-year-old hermit who'd rather hike along a stream than attend any social gathering, even a tribal celebration. He'd sneak away from his own birthday party to go out on a hill and watch the clouds. He had more affection for plants and animals than for people, any people, Indian or Anglo. He also had a quick temper around most people. A gathering of more than five was a crowd to him, and he avoided crowds.

Buffalo Sun was hard-headed, arrogant, and severe-ly opinionated, but he'd give you the shirt off his back if he liked you. I saw him do just that more than once. He made his own clothes, his tipi, and most of his tools and utensils. He was a master craftsman. He skinned and tanned all his hides and hunted or grew most of what he ate. Buffalo Sun would come down out of the mountains once every three months or so to sell his hide paintings. He'd pick up his supplies, drink a few beers, and rush back to his tipi as though just released from a prison sentence. I learned all my leather-crafting skills from living four full seasons with him. His only weaknesses that I knew of were his compulsiveness to always keep busy doing some-thing and his lack of tolerance toward people.

One time Buffalo Sun and I were placed in charge of a wilderness survival camp sponsored by a medi-cine man we were apprenticed to. A group of students from a church congregation arrived unannounced for a week's workshop. Buffalo Sun was insulted and em-phatically stated that he was not a babysitter. (He was indeed the most knowledgeable and skilled wilder-ness survival person I ever met.) He asked me to call a camp council meeting with everyone present that evening. We built a fire and offered the sacred pipe. All were in attendance, camp residents as well as our Christian visitors. After some ceremonial singing and eating, Buffalo Sun gave a thirty-minute speech on the historical travesties inflicted on Indian people by Christian missionaries. He then politely informed our Christian visitors that they were to leave in peace early the next morning. Then he walked out of the council circle. There was an attempt at discussion by our vis-itors, but I would not accept it.

I mentioned to them that what had been said by Buf-falo Sun was true, that we were not comfortable with so many Bibles around camp. I also mentioned that the last thing in the world a traditional Indian medicine camp needed was the Bible and "converting Christians." Buffalo Sun then abruptly reappeared and informed the visitors that he did not want to become a "convertible," that he was a "hard top." The next morning, all those Christian folks left camp in a caravan, with Buffalo Sun standing by the road smiling and waving good-bye. As one car drove past him, a man handed him a Bible. Buffalo Sun later tore out some pages to start his nightly fire in the tipi. This was my brother-friend, Buffalo Sun of the Lakota (Sioux) Nation. Full Night, also a Lakota, was a female image of Buffalo Sun.

I arrived in Montana in midwinter with the snow piled high. The "square house" Buffalo Sun and Full Night were wintering in was an old mill cabin, back in the woods on a creek, somewhere between Seeley Lake and the town of Kalispell. Some local people in one of the small towns pinpointed its location for me. I had to park my truck and climb up a snowbank about five feet high to see their cabin. It was situated about 500 yards across a meadow. As I walked towards it, I realized I was walking on snow which had accumulated and crusted to a depth of five feet but nevertheless was solid. The cabin was beautiful; you could tell it was "tight" and well secured for winter. The white smoke rising serenely from its chimney appeared to be etched against the blue sky.

When I was about a hundred feet away, I called out my friends' names. As I walked, I looked down toward my feet and the snow beneath me. I was expecting to sink down in a soft spot in deep snow at any time. When I looked up again toward the cabin, I saw Buffalo Sun and Full Night standing in the doorway. We ran toward one another and embraced as we hooted and hollered. Buffalo Sun had a long beard with hair down to his waist; Full Night's hair had grown beyond her waist. This made me realize how long it had been since I had seen them. The expression on their faces and in their eyes had changed. They were the healthiest looking folks I'd seen in years. But the difference about them was beyond that; there was a serene aloofness and a tranquil detachment emanating from both of them. Each wore a hand-carved wooden cross on a leather thong around the neck. I said, "You both sure look different." Buffalo Sun responded, "We are, praise God. Praise Jesus."

Inside their cabin were hides and furs hanging on the walls, over chairs, and spread out on the floor. The furniture was hand-made from lodgepole pine and willow branches. In the living room was an altar with a picture of Christ and a Bible on it. Everything was clean, orderly, and homey. I asked if they'd been reading the Bible. Buffalo Sun replied yes but he was trying to get another one because some pages were missing from his. I was in a state of near shock.

After they had served me tea, fruit, and toast, I heard their traditional Lakota blessing end with the phrase —"in the name of Jesus." Although my curiosity was overwhelming, our conversation remained in the areas of intertribal news and weather. Whenever I shared a bit of good news with them about a friend or relative, they would smile and exclaim, "Praise God."

My surprise and curiosity became too much for me to restrain. I had to inquire. I bluntly asked if they were embracing Jesus. They looked at each other and laughed heartily. Full Night said, "Jesus has embraced us!" I told them I didn't come to get converted, that I did not want to hear about the Jesus Road while visiting them. I would love them no matter what, and I asked them to respect my request. They giggled like children and agreed to honor my request.

For the next two days, I watched their every movement like a hawk. They were so happy and full of
light. They sang songs about Jesus as they went about
their daily chores. I couldn't believe it. One evening
after dinner, they asked me if it would bother me if
they read from the Bible aloud to one another. I gently
expressed that I would never interfere with their daily
routine. They took turns reading to one another with
the innocence of children. They both looked younger
and fresher. Were they really "re-born"? I had never
seen Buffalo Sun so calm and contained, nor so gentle and patient. That late winter evening as we sat
around the lantern-lit living room table with the snow
outside piled up against the cabin, I asked them what
had happened to bring about such a personal transformation.

They told me that when they first arrived in Montana they were arrogant and thought they knew everything about wilderness survival. But then the snow
came. It came every night for months and piled higher
every day. The sun would shine each day, but the tem-
perature sometimes dropped below zero for weeks.
The Chinook winds out of Canada drifted the snow
so high that they couldn't go outside to hunt or to do
anything. Each morning they had to shovel a new path
to the outhouse. They made snowshoes and used them
to walk to a frozen creek for water. They broke off tree
limbs for firewood. Some days they stayed in bed just
to keep warm.

They became cabin bound and restless and began
to argue and nag one another every day. Just to get
away for awhile one evening, Buffalo Sun decided to
snowshoe out to the road and hitch a ride to the near-
est small town. Along the way, a snowstorm blew in.
No one was on the road to give him a ride. It became
icy cold and windy. Buffalo Sun said he became so

demoralized and disgusted that he began to pray and to complain to God. He was hungry, cold, disillusioned, and just plain mad. He prayed to Grandfather Great Spirit to renew his medicine power. He prayed to be shown how to revive and freshen his spirit power.

Soon after his prayer, he saw headlights coming his way from town. A car stopped, and a middle-aged man asked him what he was doing out in a storm. Buffalo Sun told him he needed a ride into town. The man said he was coming from town and everything was closed there. Buffalo Sun decided to get a ride with this man back to the cabin.

While in the car, Buffalo Sun noticed a big, juicy hamburger on the seat between them. The man asked if he was hungry and offered him the hamburger. Buffalo Sun felt strange taking the only hamburger, but he ate it. The man asked if he was an Indian, and Buffalo Sun told him he was Sioux. The man replied that he was Arapahoe. Soon they arrived at the path to the cabin. Buffalo Sun thanked the driver for the ride and the hamburger. The man handed Buffalo Sun a small booklet, a copy of the New Testament, and he said, "Here, eat this, this is food to nourish your spirit." Buffalo Sun asked the man if he was a "Jesus freak." The man replied that he and Jesus were one. Then he drove away.

Buffalo Sun found Full Night very worried about him being out in a blizzard at night. She too had been praying to the Great Spirit to send Buffalo Sun back home safely with a new peace. He told Full Night the story about the hamburger, the Arapahoe man, and the New Testament. The words of Jesus Christ were printed in red in the booklet. They both decided to read only the red words. They took turns reading aloud the words of Jesus Christ. Over the next few weeks, they experienced a peace, comfort, and release from restlessness that they never knew before. They claimed it was the Holy Spirit. They said Jesus had saved them from their discouragement and inner turmoil and arrogance, that they experienced the love of God through accepting the compassionate Jesus in their lives. This was their story.

They were strong in their conviction. I was happy for them. I saw peace and assurance in their countenances as well as in their home. I remained with them the rest of that winter and all of spring. It snowed almost every night until May.

I, also, began reading the red words of Jesus and then also the Bible. I was amazed at the wisdom, compassion, and power of this Nazarene. The world was never the same again after his coming. One night I asked in prayer that if Jesus Christ was really the son of God become a human being, then could I see it and feel it. I was actually expecting nothing to happen! Yet within moments after the asking, I experienced the enlightenment of Christ's presence. I saw Him and touched Him. He spoke to me. I was amazed. Jesus was real.

The following morning I took a walk. My new awakening and relationship with the Great Spirit through Jesus Christ opened my eyes and heart to the difference between Christ's teaching (original Christianity) and the doctrine and dogma of organized church Christianity. God loves the world so much that he incarnated as a human being to show us that we are in his image, that we are all children of God. No longer did I view the Great Spirit as a faraway deity, but as a close relative, as a Father. What a beautiful relationship with Source, that of Father and son. Jesus in His compassionate love can become an instantaneous savior for anyone, by the asking.

That winter and spring, I studied the sacred scripture of the Bible with Buffalo Sun and Full Night. It was a time of prayer and of singing praises. It was a winter of renewal and a spring of new growth. That Easter Sunday morning, the three of us sang praises to Jesus Christ during a sweat lodge ceremony, after which I was submerged in a creek and baptized in the Holy Spirit. I do not belong to an organized church because to me modern theology does not always reflect the spirit of Jesus's teachings. But I do embrace the original Christianity as revealed by Jesus Christ and the prophets. I did not seek Jesus Christ, he sought me. He is truly a savior. To prove this to yourself, listen to people's testimonies and observe the Christ-like changes in their lives. There are today many miraculous healings occurring in the name of Jesus. Perhaps the essence of Christ's message was that anyone can become one with God, just for the asking.

For example, several years ago I counseled two young people for a while regarding their behavior problems and drug abuse. They seemed "hard-core" at the time; they were intelligent and seemed to have stubborn answers for almost everything, except for their own well-being! They eventually ran away from home, so I didn't see them for some time.

Recently both of them seemed to just appear before me downtown in Santa Fe. Their eyes were clear, their faces healthy and happy. They proudly told me that they were back home, no longer on drugs but now "on the Bible" and trying to be of service to God. I studied their faces. There wasn't a trace of extremism or fanaticism. It was real! They mentioned that they were attending Victory Chapel for fellowship and growth. I was amazed at their authentic growth and "new self."

Being the sometimes skeptic and cynic I was (especially toward churches), I went to Victory Chapel with them, more out of curiosity than to confront or challenge, because I respected the authenticity of what I saw in these two beautiful young people. I spent three hours in Victory Chapel observing, almost "studying" the details of the chapel, and especially taking note of the people there.

As time went on I was more than impressed. I found myself participating in song and in joy. (I have my weaknesses, but I am not easily fooled.) It has been some time since I've seen folks of various ages and backgrounds so full of happiness. The teenagers were considerate and respectful, gently welcoming me and seemingly committed to being complete people.

The pastor, Pastor Huch, poured forth a beautifully balanced sharing and exchange. He and his gathering were organized, clean, honest, and balanced. Pastor Huch was sincere and provocative—not watered-down or diluted in his biblical message. He was compassionate, human and humorous. He is a man of God, of Christ, who loves life and the Bible. He can laugh at himself and make us all laugh at ourselves.

Of all saints and sages, Jesus is one of the most liberating—and self-convicting. Jesus did not mean for us to feel guilty and he did not preach guilt. He expounded forgiveness. Guilt comes from inside a person; we choose to feel guilty. Jesus is also still controversial among people I know. Bring up the name of Buddha or Krishna as the topic of conversation at a gathering, and folks will casually and pleasantly discuss them. When the topic of conversation turns to Jesus Christ, however, many folks will get stirred up and often the conversation will end with the declaration, "Well, I don't want to discuss religion any more!" Most folks will be intensely for or against Jesus. You will not find such demonstrative reactions

among people toward other saints, sages, or prophets
in history as the revolutionary Nazarene, who incidentally, was a Rabbi quite unpopular among the peers
of his day.

So many of us respond to that which provokes us
as being negative, but to provoke is to cause movement—in thought, action, or perhaps in both. My
grandmother told me that life sometimes was like a
big bowl of stew. One has to keep it "stirred up" or
scum would form on top. When I see a bumper sticker
that reads, "Jesus saves," I envision a statement next
to it: "Jesus provokes."

The Native American Church is a beautiful joining
of Christ's teachings and the Red Road of earth and
sky. Original Christianity began in the wilderness.
Jesus was always going out to pray and to fast. He
taught by day but usually went away from people at
sunset to be with his Father. He often said that his
purest temples of worship were the mountains and
hills, not man-made structures. Christ's birth is celebrated near winter solstice; his resurrection is celebrated near spring equinox, demonstrating the
harmony of his being with the natural Medicine Wheel
of life. The earth is renewed with the new birth of the
Christ child each year; Christ was risen near the time
of spring equinox. Christ's resurrection is the rising
of the soul from its delusional state, of consciousness
from the tomb of ignorance, of the body from restlessness to calmness, and of the will from mechanical habits to directional freedom. The resurrection is new life
risen above death. Suffering from the fear of death is
dissolved: He has risen. He has risen in thee.

Some Christians show such a supreme love and devotion to God. I have seen the strongest faith in God
and the strongest love for his teachings among Christians. I have also experienced the most negative judg-

ments from Christians. Once in a while, Buffalo Sun, Full Night, and I would attend a church in town for awhile, because we loved to sing praise to Jesus with other people. But eventually, some church folks would begin to criticize us and claim we were "not really saved" because we didn't give up our "heathen" Indian ceremonies. I have received criticism from some Christians as not being authentically "born again." I have also received criticism from some Indians because of my relationship with Jesus Christ. This behavior reminds me that I am not here to please people but to please God, to be "in" the world, not "of" the world. Smoking the sacred pipe, sharing of breath made visible with all creation, brings me closer to Source and its incarnate Son made flesh, Jesus. Some things I have put aside in my new relationship with the Great Spirit through Jesus, for in every gain there is a loss. But I am a stronger Cheyenne because of following Christ.

The Bible is a large part of my personal conviction, which I will share with folks if requested. I realize that the truth of the Bible is universal and available for all, but it is an individual's free choice—as it was my choice. Buffalo Sun and Full Night did not try to convert me or force me. The miracles and healings of Jesus Christ were unlike any other in the history of the earth. His miracles and healings were witnessed by thousands, and recorded by many skeptical Roman historians who also witnessed those miraculous events.

Although the original Christianity of Jesus Christ and his followers began in the wilderness, its development in the following centuries was primarily urban. It became, in fact, a religion practiced in churches in towns and in cities. Although I have observed an admirable faith and love for God among my Christian brothers and sisters, most of them also seem alienated from nature and its creatures.

Original Christianity is partially an outgrowth of the teachings of the Essenes, whose love of and participation in nature has been well known throughout the ages. John the Baptist is said to have been an Essene. Few Christians realize the full significance of the type of ceremony he performed on Jesus in a river. During the centuries following Christ's death and resurrection Christianity grew progressively more alienated from nature, focusing not on God's glory manifested in the natural world but treating animals and plants as inferior and non-spiritual life forms. Nature became a force to be reckoned with or dominated, instead of a living manifestation of God to be in harmony and in balance with.

The first symbol of Christianity was not the cross but a fish. The fish suggests the presence of living water, the life-giving Source. It is also a reference to the Christian Eucharist. The peacock, the lamb, and the dove were also early Christian symbols from the natural world. Early church fathers did not prohibit the use of images and symbols, only their worship. Although images and symbols are valuable for instruction and devotion, the evolving Christian church abandoned many of them in order to separate itself from the pagan world. There was a further suspicion of art as being vain, worldly, and unspiritual. Eventually, however, the organized Christian church began to use many images and icons as it developed its doctrines and dogmas. Yet today many fundamentalist Christians accuse Native Americans of idol worship because of the use of animal, plant, and mineral symbols and images in their religious ceremonies.

Currently, there are indications of a spiritual revival

in some Christian churches worldwide. My prayer and hope is that whatever separates different denominations is cleansed and transformed by the spirit of Christ's original message. The Christian churches, as well as individual Christians, would do best to let their light shine instead of forcing their interpretations of God's designs on their neighbors. The doctrines and dogmas of Christianity should not take precedence over following the compassionate teachings of the Master, the main object for which the Gospel was written.

I needed the solitude of the spirit of winter in Montana that year to view Jesus Christ and the Bible without distraction, to distill out prejudgments and acquired bitterness. I needed quiet that I might listen. That winter with Jesus Christ and the Bible, with Buffalo Sun and Full Night, with the Northern Lights and the Chinook wind reminded me and strengthened my personal conviction that every experience holds a lesson, every encounter an insight, and every event a message. I realized anew that these things have to be made visible by practicing them in our daily lives. The invisible breath of sacred teaching becomes visible in living it out here on earth.

> The Spirit of God has made me and the Breath
> of the Almighty gives me life.
>
> (Job)

James Buffalo Sun and Lila Full Night got married and moved to a cabin near Missoula, Montana. They eventually had two children and became known as two of the most amiable and likable neighbors in town. Buffalo Sun became a professional artist. Full Night worked with children.

Before I returned to Greywolf's camp after my stay with them, I visited my sister in eastern Montana. She

danced at a powwow that summer in traditional Cheyenne native dress. Her fully beaded belt had the inscription "Jesus Saves" beaded in red letters against
a white background. I was beside myself with delight.
I spent an enjoyable afternoon with her and her new
husband, listening to tapes of them singing Cheyenne
songs and Jesus hymns. She told me she would go to
a church sometimes, but she had to keep changing
churches because often a preacher or a congregation
would ask her to stop wearing her "Indian clothes"
or to stop dancing. I told her I understood. She said
all she wanted to do was to love and praise Jesus. She
said if God didn't want her to be Cheyenne, then she
wouldn't have been born a Cheyenne. I told her not
to be concerned, that Jesus was an Arapahoe.

Late that summer, I returned to Greywolf's camp
with a renewed and expanded vision, and with a burden of bitterness and arrogance lifted from me. I had
a new relationship with the Great Spirit through Jesus
Christ. I greeted Greywolf and the camp welcoming
circle with my prayer pipe in hand and a portable Bible in my back pocket. They said that they had missed
me. They said I looked very different from when they
last saw me the previous spring. I responded, "I am
different. Praise God. Praise Jesus."

IV
The New Art of an Ancient People

To carve stone is to love it.
To go into stone and make a pipe is
to be at one with stone.

John Redtail Freesoul

17
Centuries of Pipe-Making

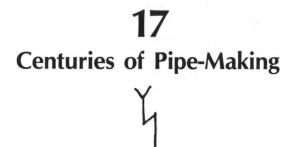

I have waited long to write about the pipe. It scares me. It is so sacred. Our elders tell us how the sacred pipe was brought to the tribes. Thunder brought the pipe to the Blackfoot; traditionally they make their pipes of black stone. The Great Spirit sent the pipe through Duck to the Arapahoe. The Lakota have beautiful White Buffalo Calf Maiden, whose story is a lesson to us all. She came with a spiritual gift for the people; when a warrior tried to possess her lustfully, he was transformed into a pile of worms by a cloud. The ancient prophet Sweet Medicine brought the arrow pipe bundle to the Cheyennes at Bear Butte.

"The pipe is more than a thing; it is alive." These words of John (Fire) Lame Deer have left a deep impression on me. My teachers have been from many tribes: Cheyenne, Arapahoe, Lakota, Blackfoot, Apache, Hopi, Nez Perce, and Iroquois. Of them, John (Fire) Lame Deer, a holy man of the Lakota tribe, taught me the most completely. The most significant lesson I learned from Lame Deer is that if one becomes visible to the public and speaks or writes about the Red Road and the sacred pipe, his life should be clean.

Being pure is not being self-righteous or "holier than thou." It is speaking straight, without ulterior motives. If one speaks or writes about the pipe, the sweat lodge, or the Medicine Wheel, he should be living the pipe, sweat lodge, and Medicine Wheel. These are to be practiced as tools of the divine, instead of reduced to marketable items for massive distribution and advertisement.

Before we are pipemakers and artists, Riverwoman and I are individual pipeholders. A pipeholder is trained and initiated to perform ceremonies with the pipe, and is bound by a code of behavior. Traditionally and spiritually observant Cheyennes will never smoke marijuana in a red pipestone pipe or any sacred ceremonial pipe. I am a man of many seasons, with Indian, Christian, and Hindu teachers, but all I do, all I might become, is as a Cheyenne-Arapahoe. I will add to my tradition, to that which has preceded me; I will never replace it.

No single pipemaker or tribe has a monopoly on the sacred pipe. Tradition varies from tribe to tribe, but the pipe is a sacred tool, object, and altar to all. It is sad when jealousy or ego surrounds the pipe, for its very essence is to promote well-being. We Cheyennes have a specific way of blessing our pipes, which I show in a pipe ceremony but will not write about. There are personal pipes, social pipes, and spiritual ceremonial pipes. Now there are pipes as art forms which we call "pipe sculpture." Although the pipes we make for sale and display in museums and galleries are authentic and functionally smokable, they are different from sacred pipes: the stem is permanently attached to the bowl. To us a pipe whose stem is detachable from the bowl is a spiritual tool, beyond being an art object. In this way we make a personal statement to our people and to the public that our

John Redtail Freesoul

Riverwoman Freesoul

sacred objects are not for sale. I have explained this to some in my tribe while in council, and they support it. We do not judge those who sell pipes with stems that detach from the bowls; we only bear witness to our own behavior. It is a personal statement. We are glad to see the Plains ceremonial pipe take its place as an art form next to the Kachina, pottery, and weavings.

As pipemakers, Riverwoman and I were proud when the Southwest Association on Indian Affairs created a new category of judging at Indian Market in Santa Fe. As a result of our artistic contribution, participation, and awards for our designs, they made a classification for "Pipes and Pipebags." But as pipeholders, we carry sacred pipe bundles and will not enter the sacred pipe in competitions. It is a great responsibility to hold a pipe bundle and perform pipe ceremonies.

Although all pipes are to promote well-being, not all pipes are "peace pipes" as designated by western folklore. There are sun dance pipes, arrow bundle pipes, marriage pipes, straight pipes, and war pipes. The leader of a war party carries the pipe as the center of power. Sometimes a pipe is used to seal a contract, as was done historically between the United States government and Indians. But we never smoked our war pipes or straight pipes with the cavalry. Once General Custer smoked a pipe with the Cheyennes, announcing peace but all the while surveying our village for an attack. The Cheyennes sensed this and emptied the ashes from the pipe bowl on Custer's boots. We all know how he was killed after attacking the Indians at Little Big Horn. I smoked my pipe with the U.S. Forest Service once when they tried to remove me from a canyon. But that's another story.

Anyone who is sincere about the pipe can pray with it. I will not initiate new pipeholders, but I will instruct some how to use a small personal prayer pipe for their private growth. To become a pipeholder and carry a long-stemmed ceremonial pipe and perform ceremonies with it for others requires years of training and preparation. One then becomes an initiate of the pipe, one who sees beyond the ordinary—not above or below others, rather beyond. If a person takes a pipe and goes alone into "the Great Silence," taking plenty of time, he or she will learn and receive a message. This can be done by anyone who has the proper attitude and is honest and sincere about his relationship with Earth Mother and Sky Father, and in following nature's rules. These things do not belong to Indians alone.

The pipe is used in almost every Plains Indian ceremony. It is the center of all we do. The first things we teach our children are the four directions of the Medicine Wheel and the pipe. The Medicine Wheel is direction. The pipe is centering, balance, and communion. It is important for children to learn direction, movement, balance, and prayer before deciding a vocation or profession. This is why the vision quest is so important. We go out alone (sometimes with a pipe) and enter a circle, to discover who we are and what is Sky Father's destiny for us. We do this before we pursue a profession.

The pipe is a tool, but it is also an altar. While used in many ceremonies, there is a specific pipe ceremony, and there are pipe dances. Sometimes a pipe ceremony is used to heal the sick.

The American Indian ceremonial pipe has been in use for centuries. The earliest pipes that have been found are simple tube pipes discovered in prehistoric mounds in Ohio. They are made of clay and alabaster. It is interesting that a most sacred type of Cheyenne pipe is our "straight pipe," which is a tubular bowl on a wooden stem. The earliest long-stemmed pipes had bowls made of animal heads, usually ducks and birds. Our bird ceremonial pipes, which are most popular with the Wheelwright Museum in Santa Fe, commemorate this beginning. Some folks where I went to college in Ohio gave me an old alabaster tube pipe they found while digging in a corn field on their farm.

The use of ceremonial pipes spread along the Mississippi River and into the lakes and eastern Plains areas around the 11th century. One of the first tribes observed by Europeans using the pipe were the Micmac of Nova Scotia. The first Europeans to record their observations of the pipe ceremony were French Jesuits, who gave the pipe the Norman name for reed—"calumet." Later the sacred red pipestone was renamed catlinite and poets wrote of "catlinite calumets."

The animal head pipes of the 15th and 16th centuries had reed stems. At that time one bowl had many stems, and the stems were more decorative and more sacred than the bowl. When a stone pipe bowl was added as an altar to the highly decorated reed stem, the combination became the revered "calumet pipe." This became a passport, symbolizing good faith and good will among Plains and Woodland tribes. Also disc pipes were carried in Osage war bundles.

The pipe traveled west among tribes in trade and migration. The Ojibwa, Plains Cree, Blackfoot, and Crow used it in modified forms, in materials such as pipestone, steatite, and sandstone. Plains pipes were made of steatite, chlorite, shale, and limestone. Northwest coast tribes carved pipes of black argillite. The most favored pipe material by far is the hard-pressed

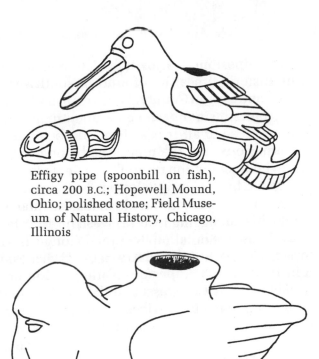

Effigy pipe (spoonbill on fish),
circa 200 B.C.; Hopewell Mound,
Ohio; polished stone; Field Museum of Natural History, Chicago,
Illinois

Effigy pipe (winged shaman), circa 200 B.C.; Ohio;
greenstone; British Museum, London

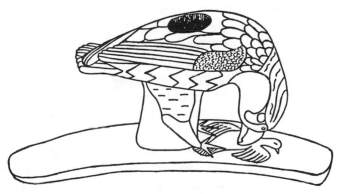

Effigy pipe, circa 200 B.C.; Ohio; after Squier. ''The sculpture is spirited and life-like, as well as minute and delicate.''
Present location unknown.

Drawings by R. Balthazar

clay-state "pipestone," known to Native Americans since prehistoric times. It is found in southwestern Minnesota and Barron County, Wisconsin. The quarry in Minnesota, now a pipestone national monument, is a sacred place to all tribes. The land belonged to the eastern Sioux, but the pipestone belonged to all Indians who honored the pipe. The quarry was probably first used by the Oto and Iowa tribes. George Catlin was the first white man to describe the quarry in print and his pipestone sample was the first to be studied. Pipestone is called "catlinite" in his honor. The eastern Sioux lost the quarry to the U.S. Government in 1928. In 1937 Pipestone National Monument was established by Congress, and the right to quarry pipestone was given to all tribes. There are many legends about this quarry. The most beautiful is that of the Omaha and Sioux, who were traditionally enemies and always at war. But at the quarry they were together in peace. Today we always give an offering before we quarry the sacred pipestone.

Originally the unfinished bowl of a pipe was sunk into a log or block of wood where it was held securely. Then it was drilled by a piece of very hard wood to make the hole the desired size. This stick or drill was then rolled between the hands, while a fine sand and water were applied to the hole in the pipe. In finishing the bored hole, a second person pressed on top of the drill with another block of wood to prevent vibrating. Great precision was gained, but much labor and patience were required.

Stems were made of any wood that had a soft, pithy center. Hot wire was used to push out the pith. The smoke channel was also created by splitting hard wood such as ash, oak, or hickory into two halves, scraping the pith out, and regluing the pieces. For glue, the sticky secretions from boiled buffalo cow hooves were often used. The route along which the smoke was conducted was a secret of the artisan. These items were called "puzzle stems," and they added to the mystery of the pipe. Round stems were common to Plains tribes. The stone was polished with beeswax, and lead or pewter was used in inlay to decorate or to repair broken bowls.

There are a variety of forms of pipes. There are tube pipes, elbow pipes, "T" pipes, platform pipes, disc pipes, straight pipes, tomahawk pipes, and effigy pipes. The word "tomahawk" is from the Algonquin *tomahakan,* meaning "axe." Recently, I designed a "hawk-in-flight" ceremonial pipe on a wood base. When in use as a pipe, the design is that of a tomahawk pipe. When placed on the pipestand the design is that of a hawk in flight, a pipe sculpture. I call it my "hawk-tomahawk" pipe, which commemorates the original tomahawk pipes. The tomahawk pipes became popular as trade items among mountain men. There are also phalliform pipes. A ritual transfer of sacred power can be effected through intercourse between male and female. Tubular pipes sometimes symbolized the male power. Sioux members of the Grand Medicine Society carved the effigy pipes representing the male creative power. Some pipe bowls represent the symbolic transfer between male and female power.

Ceremonial pipes were carved in the 16th and 17th centuries with several figures (animal and human) on a stone stem, as well as on a stone bowl elaborately inlaid with metal. Some of these stylized pipes are known as "platform effigy pipes." A flat platform was shaped on the stone bowl. On this a social or religious statement was depicted by one or more animal or human figures, sometimes both. Or an animal spirit guide was represented on the platform. These figures usually faced the smoker. Later in the 1800s the carved figures usually faced the part of the bowl in which the tobacco was burned, which represents the center of the universe and the same fire as the sun. Most of the designs River and I create are similar to this style.

In speaking of traditional pipes, most folks refer to the elbow L or T pipes of the mid-19th century as their point of reference and yardstick of comparison. Some of these pipes were inlaid with metal and had carved figures on them, usually only one on the bowl and none on the stem. It was at this time that contact with the Europeans was rising and the Indian wars began. Consequently, tribes were on the move more (and rapidly), and the simple L and T shaped bowl with quillwork stems became popularized. Later, in the beginning of the 20th century, tourist "peace pipes" came into being. Whether or not a pipe is traditional depends on which century in Indian history one uses as a point of reference. Also, a pipe may be traditional Plains, but not traditional Woodland, Great Lakes, or Northwest.

In the last ten years some native artists and traditional pipeholder artists have developed the ceremonial pipe as an art form in the realm of fine art. With the addition of our stone pipestands on hardwood "pipe bases," Riverwoman and I have extended the traditional ceremonial pipe into the realm of sculpture, designated by some art critics as "pipe sculpture." Some folks say our artwork is traditional, some claim it's contemporary, and some say it is a combination of both. We let the dialogue continue; it is sad when artists are ignored.

Several years ago at the Indian Market in Santa Fe, our designs were criticized as being too ornate for traditional Plains Indian art. Our friend Helen Hardin, Tsa-sah-wee-eh to the Indians, was displaying her

paintings across from our booth. Two years previously, we had traded a pipe and pipe bag to Helen for
a painting. She was an elegant woman, a provocative
artist who inspired movements of growth and awareness in people through her art. People agreed or dis-
agreed with her, but no one was indifferent to her.
Her deep convictions about life always brought out
a response, and when she spoke people unconsciously
hunched forward to listen closer.

That summer when I was criticized, Helen told me
to "be sensitive to" but not to become "vulnerable
to" public opinion and response. She said, "If you
are a free artist, then create what you see, do what you
want." Her words strengthened my personal vision
and brought me a new realization. They have remained a source of encouragement.

Helen Hardin's spirit has now left her body, but her
presence during Indian market under the portal of the
Palace of the Governors will remain strong. I will continue to see her there across from my booth, smiling
and looking upward to the blue sky and the sun.

River and I are careful with what we do with the
pipe as artists. We are pipeholders before we are artists. We will add to our tradition but never replace
it. Thus we enhance and extend our roots as does a
flowering tree. Sculpting is a personal and special-
ized craft and art. We are guided by tradition, but we
experiment freely, yet respectfully, to create unique
conceptions from imagination, spiritual vision, and
from observing and contemplating nature and its four
seasons.

18
Earth Mother's Gift of Materials

Y

I literally love the materials I use in my artwork. I use wood, bone, antler, animal hides, feathers, claws, and stone hand polished with grit and water, in sun on earth beneath sky and moon. Sometimes I use fire to polish when I bake pipestone for a glaze. With the materials I use and the elements I incorporate, I feel like an alchemist transforming separated components into a living whole. It is a sacred thing I do.

Most of our ceremonial pipes are of pipestone. It is *lila wakan*—very sacred, the most sacred stone for pipes. This is what Riverwoman and I started carving with and it is my favorite carving stone. It is harder than alabaster and less temperamental—it fractures less from heat and pressure than any other carving stone. It is the color of blood and of red earth, often speckled with white dots and swirls, simulating stellar constellations such as the Milky Way. Staring deep into the matrix of pipestone can take you far away. Many Indians call pipestones *inyan-sha* (red stone) or *shatunka* (red sacred strong stone). The Sioux also use a black pipestone which is special in its own way.

Like other forms of life, rock is male or female. Most alabaster is female. We use it to carve the female aspects of hawks and eagles, and it helps us bring forth the mystery and awe of the female power in life and the medicine of the white buffalo. It is a mystical stone used by ancient tribes the world over for medicinal vases, amulets, and pipes.

The alabaster we use for pipes is from the quarry originally found and developed in Italy by Michelangelo. This Italian alabaster is found with "statuare," the highest grade marble in nature. It is without impurities or inclusions. This renders it dense and uniform for carving and safe for smoking.

The beauty of this stone is awe-inspiring. One cannot help but carve something of sheer beauty and elegance out of translucent white Italian alabaster. It absorbs light and reflects it and seems to glow from within. Of all the types of stone I carve, Italian white alabaster is the most ethereal, the most mystical, resembling moonstone. It appears cold as ice, yet is warm to the touch. I often wonder what Michelangelo's reaction would be to an Indian in America carving ceremonial pipes out of a stone that he developed and popularized.

We also use Utah alabaster, with red, green, and yellow mixture of colors often resembling the colors of Earth Mother during autumn, of golden aspen against a perennial evergreen background. This alabaster is a favorite among many Native American stone sculptors, such as Presley La Fontaine and his brother Bruce La Fontaine. Another favorite is Colorado alabaster, ranging from white to pink and resembling the color of smoked salmon. It is nicknamed "salmon alabaster." Oklahoma marble and alabaster have a red and purple rose-like matrix against a white back-

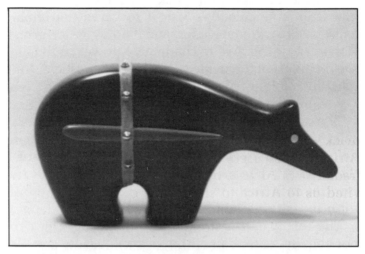

Bear spirit fetish, African wonderstone

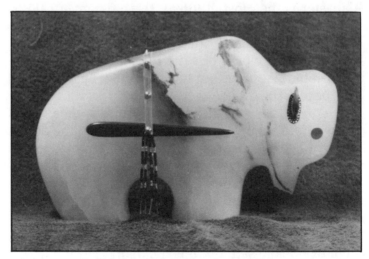

Buffalo spirit fetish, Italian alabaster

ground. Kiowa sculptor Ted Creepingbear and I introduced this stone to Santa Fe in 1982. When polished, its natural matrix design often simulates that of wild mountain flowers against a snow-covered meadow. These natural matrixes of the stone are Mother Nature's inlay.

We also carve wonderstone, which is found in East Africa and in the state of Washington. It is gray or black with some blood-red color. It is the stone many African tribes use for pipes. Originally, River and I traded with African bead traders for it, and they invited us to Africa to share pipe ceremonies.

Black wonderstone is a masculine stone. Like argillite, it is a compact clay-stone. Its dense uniformity and consistency of solid makeup make it a stone carver's delight. This stone holds fine lines of detail and can take a luster of polish approaching obsidian. With five to ten coats of treewax, wonderstone can become as black as jet. Silver discs inlaid in highly polished black wonderstone provide an elegant contrast of light and dark, as a full moon on a dark and starless night.

We use a variety of woods for pipe stems and bases for pipes and sculptures. The aroma of the cedar, cherry, walnut, oak, and ash is as purifying and refreshing as any incense. The texture and grain of these woods deepen with time as they are handled and polished with the natural oils of the hand. Recently we have started using imported hardwoods such as shadua, Brazilian rosewood, paduk, and British Guianan mahogany. We polish both wood and stone with neatsfoot oil, bear grease, treewax and beeswax, rubbed by hand with buckskin. The stone is hand polished with silicone carbide grit mixed with water.

Pipes for spiritual use in tribal ceremonies are made entirely by hand without electricity. They are hand drilled, hand carved, and hand polished. The only electricity we use for any pipe is for drilling and for grinding or cutting large boulders into preforms. We quarry most of our stone or trade for it. River and her two sisters sometimes go to Minnesota for a load of pipestone.

We begin making sacred pipes with a sweat lodge ceremony, and we smoke our studio and equipment with cedar and sweet grass. We rarely accept money for them. A gift or services rendered in our behalf are more appropriate for the exchange of such pipes. Lame Deer told me years ago, "Take care of the pipe, and the pipe will take care of you."

In preparing religious ceremonial pipes it is good to pay attention to the phases of the sun and moon and the equinoxes and solstices. We usually begin our work day in the studio at sunrise with a tobacco cere-mony. (Our studio faces the East.) The pipe I am work-ing on now for Chief Archie Blackowl of the Southern Cheyennes in Oklahoma was started on a new moon. The specific power at certain times in nature is chan-neled through the artist "into" the item being made, but power also comes "to" the artist from the item being made. To the unenlightened, such practice is labeled superstitious and pagan; to the enlightened it is understood as an attunement to God's law mani-fested in nature. We respect creation but worship only the Creator. This is why we use such materials in our art.

In addition to stone carvings, we make leather ob-jects, such as shields. There are different kinds of shields among Plains tribes—clan, society, war, and vision shields. War shields were small and thick, usually made from the neck of a buffalo bull, to repel arrows and musket balls. Clan and society shields displayed on a tripod outside a tipi announced one's social affiliations. A vision shield was a portrayal of one's medicine power received from one's personal vision or given by a shaman or medicine person. Crazy Horse had black and white hailstone medicine. Roman Nose had water medicine, as his strongest vision resulted from fasting and praying on a raft in the middle of a lake for four days and four nights. Sitting Bull had sitting buffalo bull medicine, shown in symbol and color on his shield as a huge buffalo bull sitting upright, steadfast, secure, and unmoving.

I have developed what is called a "dream shield." It is an extension of the traditional vision shield. A dream shield represents a person's dream and highest aspirations of life. When someone relates a dream or shares a personal vision with me, I can begin his or her dream shield. The dream or vision may involve a symbol, an animal, or a plant. Often certain rocks, crystals, shells, or beads, and shaped pieces of metal are suspended beneath the circular shield among the hanging fringe. Sometimes religious pendants are hung in the fringe, with locks of hair or tied cloth bundles of sage or tobacco. Spiritually such a shield is powerful; artistically it is beautiful to see a waterfall effect of these items hanging among twisted fringe two or three feet long beneath the shield. I encourage folks to add or take away items on their dream shield as their dreams and visions change and grow. Sometimes folks must take away or release to make room for new growth.

Some dream shields, like my own, represent an extension of the higher self. Dream shields are our highest vision and can represent the best things about us. They therefore can assist us in striving to make our dreams more real, as well as to protect and sustain existing dreams in a mundane world. Dream shields were useful tools in art therapy when I was a professional therapist.

Sometimes we make a pipe, pipebag, and shield set, with dream or medicine symbols in contrasting or complementary designs. My "medicine wheel shield set" is popular. It consists of four shields, each depicting the animal, plant, color and specific medicine of each of the four directions of the Medicine Wheel. Making dream shields often is a rewarding and cleansing experience for me. Sometimes I make marriage shields as well. Dream shields can also commemorate an event such as a marriage or a baptism. Once I made a shield for a rabbi's son's coming of age. It had ancient Hebrew symbols from the Kabbalah on it. I learned much about Hebrew mysticism those weeks I sat in consultation with the rabbi. And he learned about Plains Indian dream shields.

The hides we use for our pipebags and dream shields are hand tanned, which renders them softer and more durable. Commercial tanning breaks down animal fibers quickly with chemicals, making a hide weak and too dry.

The paint colors I use are all earth colors—black, white, red, yellow, brown, or green. They are never bright. Sometimes I use blue, but I am careful because blue is a very sacred color to Cheyennes. We use it only to represent Blue Sky, the Creator. It is also one of our sacred sun dance colors. I mix my paint with natural pigment and stone dust, sometimes with bear grease to make it more waterproof. Mixing paint involves attention, prayer, and ceremony. This is the only way I do it, even though it takes time. My art is beyond being a career and a means of acquiring income. My art is my life—financially, spiritually, and vocationally. This is the way it all started.

Buffalo-eagle dream shield

Magpie ceremonial pipebag

It is a healing and a purifying experience for me to create and to bear witness to the living Great Spirit. It is a privilege to be a channel for the creative spirit of God flowing from sky to earth and from earth to sky. Our art is made in the name of the living God and in the name of our people.

Riverwoman and I are proud to be pipe artists. When folks see us, they think of the pipe. The pipe is still alive as a ceremonial tool and an art form. The pipe is forever contemporary. We are the new art of an ancient people. Today the sacred pipe is used in spiritual ceremonies, in counseling, in communicating, in sealing contracts, as a tool of self-realization and as a unique art form displayed in museums and galleries. The pipe expands as a flowering tree, from one century to the next. So be it.

Men like Old Bear and Dull Knife looked westward; where the full moon stood on the land, and remembered what had happened on each of the streams they were passing. Things that would always be a part of the today there in the Cheyenne pattern of time.*

*From *Cheyenne Autumn* by Mari Sandoz. Copyright (c) renewed 1981 by Caroline Pifer. Reprinted by permission of McIntosh & Otis, Inc.

19

Visions and Inspiration

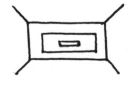

The "pipe way" is our art, our religion, and our life. People ask us about our inspiration; where do we get ideas? All our lives Riverwoman and I have lived in the country, close to nature. Nature is truly our teacher. Nature is color, symmetry, balance, harmony, and line. We watch the lines, the symmetry, the designs in clouds, mountains, earth formations, and the changes of the seasons. The natural matrix of pipestone, alabaster, and marble is nature's inlay. The veins in leaves, the colors of birds, and the texture of trees are the epitome of design. And design is very important. Once I find my lines, I can design. Sometimes the stone I carve gives me the lines; sometimes I have to struggle to find them. To carve stone is to love it; to make a pipe is to be at one with stone.

As the female aspect of the Great Spirit, nature guides and embraces me as a mother encourages a child in his creative endeavors. Only God the Great Spirit truly "creates." As an artist, I connect with God's creative spirit within me and merely assemble or arrange that which has already been created by the Great Spirit, the Source of all created things. Nonetheless, I am blessed as an artist with the ability to assemble and to arrange created things around me in my unique way. The "best" in artwork may come and go according to "who's hot and who's not," but the truly unique artist can make a statement for a long time, as does a classic piece of art. My strength and talent as a creative person is my uniqueness and also my intimate relationship with nature.

One of my dearest blessings and strength in life is to participate in the creative process. I read somewhere that the creative process has three aspects: idea, energy, and power. The creative idea is the initial seed of inspiration in one's mind and spirit; the creative energy is the talent or force enabling this idea to be transformed from speculative idea to tangible reality; and the creative power is the effect the finished work of art has on folks who behold it. All three parts of this creative process are essential and interdependent for the circle of creativity to be complete. I am proud to be involved in this trinity of power as a way of life, for my art is my life and my life is my art.

When I relate that nature is my teacher and inspiration, I am speaking literally, not merely using poetic metaphor. Most of my life, I have lived away from the sensory bombardment of activity and noise of large towns and cities. Therefore, I can open up to instead of shutting out the sights and sounds surrounding me.

I usually begin work in my studio before or at sunrise with the morning star. Sometimes special projects begin on a new moon or a full moon. There is power and personality in the creative spirit of the phases of sun and moon. I have a personal relationship with the power and personality of sun and moon. The rising sun presents a new light and a fresh beginning. As dawn's first rays appear over the mountains in front of my studio, I feel a creative urge to begin; something inside me moves and the time to start has come.

My studio faces east. The power of the East and of the rising sun is that of the golden eagle, whose creative vision is beyond mere linear eyesight—it is seeing with the intuitive eye of the soul. This is circular vision, beyond linear limitation. I burn cedar and sweet grass to purify my studio with smoke for a new day of creating. I raise my arms to greet the sun and the morning star. I call upon the power of these creative forces of the East to motivate, to guide, and to teach me. Through such sincere acknowledgment and personal conversation with nature, I communicate with and make a covenant with the power of her creative wisdom. Grandfather Great Spirit is my god and Grandmother Earth is my Goddess. Faith is involved in my personal relationship with God and Goddess, but its power is the reality which I perceive and experience.

I go out regularly, alone or with a friend, to observe nature and to behold her natural cathedral. I contemplate nature's process of change and color. Many times I receive ideas and designs for pipes and sculptures from cloud formations. Once I struggled for an hour to find an idea to begin carving a block of white marble. I stopped wrestling with it and decided to take a walk and relax in detachment. While walking, I saw the outline of a white buffalo hunched, with feet forward as if charging, forming distinctly out of thunderhead clouds over the northern horizon. I returned quickly to my studio and drew this outline on the marble block. Within hours, I had carved out a splendid white buffalo bull pipe bowl. Lines, balance, symmetry, and design are most important to me in my artwork, and nature is laden with these. Once I find the

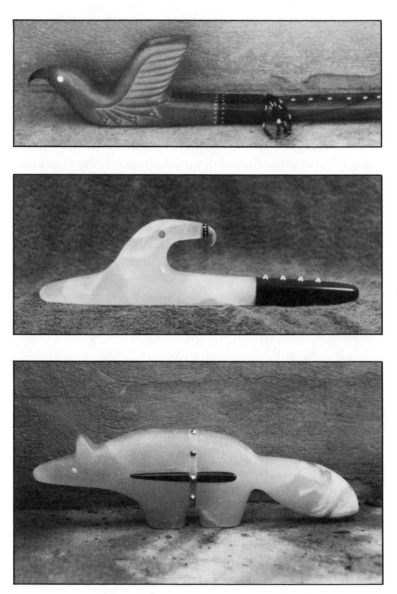

Pipes and fetish by Riverwoman and John Freesoul

lines for a particular design, I'm well on my way and flowing; sometimes finding those lines is easy and sometimes difficult. Nature is my helper in finding these lines, as well as my comforter when I can't find them.

Often just sitting in my studio and observing and touching materials—stone, bone, antler, hand-tanned hides—inspires me to begin working or experimenting with sketches of form and design. My sketch book is an important tool. I keep it in my truck while traveling because I may see a cloud formation or a striking mountain, hill, or earth arrangement, and I'll record its lines as they appear at the time. When I return to my studio, I'll sit alone and study these lines, sketching and arranging them into designs that may be different from what I originally observed. I once visited Apache master sculptor Allan Houser on the Jicarilla Apache Reservation in Dulce, New Mexico. I discovered that he values and uses his sketch book in the same way, only he experiments with the lines he observes in nature back at his studio with clay as well as in sketches on paper. I value Allan Houser's humility and master talent, as I also do that of his son, Bob Haozous; they are both the humble giants of native stone sculpture.

Sometimes a creative idea or design is brought to me in a dream. In dreams, we can be less distracted and more relaxed and able to perceive more accurately and calmly a creative vision or idea. In one of my most productive dreams I was out on the Great Plains somewhere in the Dakotas. I was alone out there on a hot sunny day with the sky as blue as the gemstone lapis lazuli. In the distant horizon, I saw a dark speck, which suddenly moved and started toward me. I noticed that it was red and traveling with great speed. As the speck approached, the ground beneath me thundered and trembled. Soon I saw that it was a red buffalo, the biggest buffalo bull I had ever seen! It was an unusually deep red color and was galloping in slow motion toward me. As it approached to within about twenty feet of me, it turned broadside and skidded, stopping abruptly. This red buffalo just stood there, sideways, in full profile view, looking at me, breathing heavily. Its breath sounded like a steam engine.

The hump of this buffalo was taller than me; I was looking up at it. Yet somehow I saw a deep hole in the top of its hump, tapered and funneled like the carved hole in a pipe bowl. I thought to myself, "Is this a living pipe?" All was quiet and still as if frozen in time. There was I and this buffalo just "being there," together, looking at one another. A voice from the sky, as if a megaphone from above, said, "This is my creation in whom I am well pleased." I woke up immediately, but I was disappointed because I wanted the dream to continue.

That morning was sunny, with a crisp blue sky. After morning prayer, I got up and went directly to my studio and drew the profile of that buffalo on a piece of deep red pipestone. The next two days, I carved a red buffalo pipe bowl and inlaid it with blue lapis lazuli. The hole for the bowl was in the buffalo's hump as in my dream, and its eyes were silver discs inlaid in red pipestone. It was the most powerful buffalo I had ever carved. The response of galleries, museums, and the public was strong. I called it "Earth-Sky Buffalo, the Power of the Plains." Whenever I look at the photograph of that buffalo pipe, I relive the dream that brought it to me. It is good to carve out my dreams in stone. It is good to share my dreams in creativity.

Often I am encouraged artistically by a manifested phenomenon in nature, which can be a direct message or affirmation from the Great Spirit. This happened the first time I attempted to carve something other than a stone pipe. This was years ago when a Crow Indian artist friend of mine, Earl Biss, was going through painful personal problems. This was interfering with his creativity and affecting his health. I had an all-night session of talking and listening to Earl at his studio. The following dawn, I was moved to begin carving a mother crow holding a newborn baby crow in her wings, extending her young upward above her head, as if raising it toward sky in prayer offering.

As I drove home to my studio that morning, across the country dirt roads north of Santa Fe, the rays of the early sun were steadily rising. I was progressively receiving the alertness to go into my studio instead of to bed. In my mind, I saw the lines and design for this crow sculpture drawn on a fine block of black African wonderstone. The symmetry of the design was upright and circular or oval. The mother crow seemed to be standing upright, arched, and leaning back, with her newborn held high in her wings above her head. She and her newborn were facing one another, eye to eye, beak to beak, almost touching. I perceived much energy in the tiny space between the two beaks, more power and energy than if they actually touched. It was the same kind of power flowing between God and Adam in Michelangelo's painting of the creation—the Creator's hand fully extended toward Adam's outstretched hand, their fingers close, almost but not quite touching.

The realization and implication of this new design gradually unfolded in my mind and spirit. I saw a circle of power of new birth and rebirth existing between a fully matured crow and her infant newborn. This mother crow represented nurturing and an affectionate, embracing, and touching kind of love. This is purifying and renewing, strong enough to bring forth new life, a biological new life as well as a life made new by psychological cleansing and a spiritual renewal. Her female love was always there, ready to touch and to nurture new growth. She held her newborn above her head, higher than herself. Mother and newborn appeared as if about to kiss, yet not touching. The energy flows in eternal process. If they were touching, the act would be over. This design seemed to represent eternal hope, the promise that we are not created and cast adrift in a sea of despair. We are held in the wings of flight of that which has preceded us, and we are capable of a continuing renewal. I saw a circle of birth, rebirth, and renewal.

The eye of the mother crow was an inlaid silver disc to represent the full moon and the fullness of maturity and complete growth. The eye of the newborn was inlaid black jet to represent the new moon and new growth. The full realization unfolded that the infant crow was more than a new biological offspring; it was also the matured crow renewed so completely that she was reborn.

I did not feel comfortable about counseling or advising my Crow Indian brother from Montana. Yet a strong and vivid intuitive movement of spirit told me that morning that this crow sculpture would help him. So I decided to begin work immediately and to dedicate it to Earl. It would be my first attempt at a stone carving in a form other than a pipe, and it would be the first time I ever dedicated my artwork to anyone.

I felt a strong directive of spirit to do something helpful for Earl Biss, to give back to him some of what he had given to me. Although he and I had just met and were not close, his paintings and creative designs inspired me as a stone carver, even more than any artist who carves stone. Earl Biss magnificently blends romantic impressionism with traditional native North American Indian mysticism. He is many things to many people. To me Earl Biss is a Native American Renoir and Matisse. He is a master artist setting the trend for other artists.

When I arrived at my studio that early summer morning, it was bright, sunny, and unusually still. Ordinarily at this time of day, there are many magpies and bluebirds fluttering around among the cedar and pinon bushes in front of my studio. That morning I did not see or hear a single bird. After I smudged myself and the studio with cedar and sweet grass smoke, I carefully recited the sun dance prayer to the Great Spirit while facing the sun. I swung open the two large studio doors and decided to begin working on the crow design, my first sculpture, outside in front of the studio, beneath blue sky and sun. I carried out a large block of black wonderstone and put it on a heavy wooden work table. It was getting warmer outside now on this August morning, so I took my clothes off and sprayed myself with cold water from the garden hose. My whole body became flushed with fresh blood. Then the warm sun began to bake my head, shoulders, and back. The combination of the cold water rinse and warm sun always has a calming effect on me.

I took my masonry saw and began to saw on the block of wonderstone to cut out the preform for the crow mother and her newborn. At that moment a large crow flew up from the west of my studio, the rear, as if it had taken off from the ground in back of the studio. It landed on top of a cedar bush and remained there for a few moments, about ten feet above the ground and thirty or so feet away. Then it began circling clockwise directly overhead, low, only about thirty feet above me. The crow cawed loudly as it circled.

Everything seemed still and quiet, as if frozen in time, as it was in my dream when I saw the red buffalo on the plains. The crow continued cawing and circling, and now it was looking down at me. I raised my right hand in a greeting of peace and acknowledgment and called out, "Ho, chinyeh, ho wanbli sapa" (Hello, brother, hello little black eagle). The crow continued to circle and caw for about ten minutes. Then it landed on a tall elm tree in back of the studio. It looked straight down at me and cawed. I saw its eyes, and the sound of its cawing echoed as if in a chamber. I raised my hand again to the little big-crow brother. As I resumed sawing the block of wonderstone, the crow flew away from the West toward the North. As I worked on the crow sculpture throughout the day, periodically I would hear a caw somewhere out in the distant brush. But I never saw brother black eagle again that day.

I finished my first sculpture that week and mounted it on a gray granite base. I mounted a pipestone plaque on the base with the carved inscription:

CROW NEWBORN REBORN

Dedicated to Earl Biss

Artist, Friend, and Crow Indian

by John Redtail Freesoul

It was displayed on a pedestal, under glass, at the Santa Fe Festival of the Arts in 1981. A family from Southern California who collected Earl's work bought that crow newborn-reborn sculpture. I heard that Earl saw a photograph of it. That same year, Earl left Santa Fe. He rearranged his life, sorted out his problems, and started a new studio in Colorado. Just a year later in August I saw Earl at a gallery opening. He looked younger and healthier. He was happy.

Since then I have gained recognition and acceptance as a sculptor as well as a pipemaker. I went on to carve bears, buffalos, eagles, turtles, otters, ermines, and other animals. I developed my northern Plains style of southwestern fetish which I call "spirit fetishes." They have come to rival the acceptance and popularity of my ceremonial pipes. Years later, in 1984, I received a third-place award in sculpture for a large white Italian alabaster bear, and Riverwoman won first place in the miniature sculpture category with a pipestone bear fetish carving. Both awards were given by the Southwestern Association on Indian Affairs at that year's annual Indian market in Santa Fe.

The experience of making that crow newborn-re-born sculpture had a life of its own, and its effects seemed magical. It linked Earl Biss and me as brothers on a spiritual plane. For Earl, it represented a new life in Colorado and a renewed strength; for me it brought a new art form and expanded the horizons of my career as an artist. I will always be proud to be a pipemaker; it is my first love and commitment. But since that all-night "crow visit" with Earl Biss in his Santa Fe studio, and the "crow vision visit" the next morning at my studio in the Northern foothills outside Santa Fe, I have become a sculptor as well as a pipemaker. This is the first time I have shared this crow vision experience. It is testimony to an inspiration from another artist whose medium of expression is different from mine. It is also one of many personal examples of actual manifestations in nature used by the Great Spirit to communicate, affirm, and encourage an artist who chooses to be, above all, a son of Earth Mother and Sky Father.

The animals I carve are not exact representations,

as is in realism, nor are they totally abstract. My bears are clearly bears and my buffalos are decidedly buffalos. My style borders between abstract and realistic. I call it impressionistic or neo-impressionism. The carved image of an animal, plant, or person commemorates and calls attention to its medicine power or spiritual message, which is beyond normal sight. The eyes of my animals do not have distinct pupils or color but appear as "openings." They are always designed as holes which yield the mystical effect of a mask being worn by a power inside looking out. Sight is the bridge between inner and outer life. In my stone carvings, I usually use silver or brass discs inlaid in stone as eyes. The silver represents the moon and the brass represents the sun. The moon is female, and the sun is male. There is male and female in everything created. The Great Spirit is male and female. I use jet inlay as eyes to signify the new moon, usually for young animals.

Perhaps one must view my work with "shanta ista," the intuitive part of the heart. Perhaps even casual exposure to my work or other artistic expression may open an individual's shanta ista. Throughout the years, folks who own my work have shared personal incidents like the following: "I gave one of your bear spirit fetishes to my uncle, and he stopped getting drunk soon after." A lawyer in San Francisco writes in a letter, "My office has never been the same since your white eagle has been on my desk. Can I visit you in Santa Fe? Can we meet and talk? It feels good but I want to learn more about it." An obstetrician in Oklahoma City writes, "My patients experience a relaxing calmness when viewing your baby otter sculpture displayed in my waiting room. They are always asking me detailed questions about the meaning of its incised symbols. Can you send me some information about it so I can type its story on a card and include it as part of my display?''

Galleries have this same request. All my pipes and carvings have a story. It is my sacred responsibility as an artist to call attention to, and sometimes to magnify, the subtle beauty and provocative meaning of the spirit of life, whether it appears hidden in symbolism in the quietude of plants and rocks, or is gloriously conspicuous in the flight of a golden eagle.

V
The Prophecy of
Purification

20
Pipes and Poems

In 1972-73 after spending an eight-month winter of being snowed in up at the Mission Range above Seeley Lake, Montana, I decided to go down to Missoula to try my fortune in the city. I wanted to sell my newly tanned hides and some artwork. I arrived on a weekend in spring and left many months later.

Missoula and its seeming comforts and city conveniences caught me in a web of unforeseen surprises. I became the proprietor of a shop and trading post in partnership with a trader named Buffalo. He was the "spittin' image" of General Custer; I had long braids, an earring in each ear, and was dressed in skins and leather. You can imagine the profile he and I projected.

Buffalo wrote poems and I made pipes, so he named the shop "Pipes and Poems." We sold stone pipes, tobaccos from around the world, Mexican sandals, and Indian-made jewelry consigned by elder women from the Flathead and Blackfoot reservations. I made many bone crosses for those women, who taught me about them. It was "big medicine" for them.

205

I was a proprietor in the big city, so I bought a 1952 white Cadillac ambulance and converted it into a camper. My dog Cheena and I lived in it. When I was in a hurry to get across town, I would flash its red lights, and traffic would pull over and let me pass.

My time in Missoula held surprises for me. It was a sacred time and also a stormy time. I realized soon why I had left the Mission Range, home of the Flathead Indians and the grizzly, to come to Missoula, the pleasant valley. Isolated in Montana, I had not known that it was the time of the "second" Wounded Knee, the 1972-73 occupation of Wounded Knee. Indian leaders spearheaded the movement to get the U.S. Government to honor previous agreements that declared Indian tribes were capable of governing themselves through tribal governments. The Indians wanted harassment by federal agents on the reservation to cease. For these and other concerns, spiritual leaders from many tribes organized a takeover of Wounded Knee, which is a sacred area on the Pine Ridge Sioux Reservation in South Dakota, a site that had been desecrated in disrespect for years. Wounded Knee is the site where in 1890 the U.S. cavalry shot and killed Sioux Chief Bigfoot and his entire band, burying them in a single mass grave. This was done because they nonviolently performed the ghost dance.

Some of my friends and former teachers were at the occupation of Wounded Knee; some elders were there; women were there. They were all ready to die for the cause. The Crow Indians from Montana traveled to Wounded Knee. They shot over the heads of the Sioux and left. In this manner they showed respect for their traditional warrior enemies.

Sweat lodges were erected in and around Missoula for prayer and ceremonies for Wounded Knee. One sweat lodge was erected under the Higgins Avenue

Bridge, on the river in downtown Missoula. Pipe ceremonies were taking place all over. Many tribes were pulling together. It was a massive spiritual revival.

We used our shop and trading post as a drop-off for food, clothing, and money to go to Wounded Knee. American Indian movement members hid three warrior brothers and a sister in my shop for three days and two nights. They had left Wounded Knee to come to a powwow in Missoula and raise money, food, and clothing. Then they returned to Wounded Knee. I hung blankets in the storefront windows of my shop with a "closed" sign on the door for three days while we hid them. Some F.B.I. men were walking up and down Higgins Avenue. During those days I met a doctor who flew his plane over Wounded Knee and dropped food to the occupying warriors. I was told by Indian activists that if I was alive and Indian, then I was a member of the American Indian movement.

During that period Albert Tall Bull died. He was medicine chief of the northern Cheyennes. I was invited to his giveaway, but I never found out about it because I had been away in my mountain retreat. There was big trouble in California, too, between the Forest Service and the Pit River Indians. There was trouble above Sacramento where a bartender had shot an unarmed Indian college student to death in a bar. He was not even charged! Some brothers of my clan were at Sacramento leading a massive funeral march on the state capital. Mad Bear Anderson of the Iroquois was there. And some of my clan brothers, I discovered, were at Wounded Knee. During this time new warrior societies came into being. Sun dances were being done the old way; young men (and women) were going alone into the hills to make medicine and prayer. There were rumors of the ghost dance being revived. All this was the fulfillment of the "prophecy of purification" that I had heard of since I was a child.

From then on I knew I no longer could be apart from the struggles of my people in our isolated place in nature. Although I eventually left the city of Missoula and resumed living in my cabin and tipi, I learned I could be "in" the world and not "of" the world. After Wounded Knee I continued with my artwork, but traveled to many reservations to counsel, to teach, to be of service. I have already related many of my activities. I went to Pitt River and taught high school. I went to Hopi Third Mesa, in Arizona, and helped the Hopis try to prevent development of the San Francisco Peaks. I became employed as a professional therapist and worked for years with Indian alcoholics, using the pipe. As a result of this (and more), I was initiated as a pipeholder, and initiated into the Redtail Hawk Society, and later became the leader of this society in the Southwest. I joined the Native American Church and had a traditional peyote tipi on my land for years.

I will always live out in the country, close to Earth Mother. But I will be aware of the struggles of my people, remaining in touch to be of service. Now is the time of nonviolence. The time of the gun and rifle is over. The time of medicine power is here. We are in the time of purification. There are those who remain bitter and angry over that which is no more. There are those who are joyously, and peacefully, making new medicine and reviving old medicine. The purification brings renewal and new growth. We have a different kind of spider-trickster enemy now: drugs, alcohol, ignorance, poverty. And we are armed with the lance of the spirit.

21

A Time of
Cleansing and Healing

A "Prophecy of Purification" is coming forward today. It is a time of unification. Medicine people and
spiritual elders of most tribes in North America, and
some in South America and from Tibet, are coming
forth and bearing witness to it. The prophecy is that
representatives from tribes and religions will come
together in a sharing and an exchange of valuable spiritual tools for cleansing and for healing. The Indian
Prophecy of Purification has its counterpart in the
Christian religion, described in the Book of Revelation in the Bible. Spirit-filled Christians refer to this
prophecy as "the Return." The time for fulfillment
of this prophecy is now.

One of the many spokespersons for the Prophecy
of Purification is Grandfather David Monongyne of the
Hopi people. The Hopi are in the forefront of this prophecy. A pictograph on Prophecy Rock in Hopiland
illustrates that humankind is currently at a crossroads.
We will be either spiritually transformed or consumed
by impure actions that we have committed, both
against ourselves internally and toward the environment externally. These are beautiful yet dangerous

times. The earth is renewing and purifying itself regardless of the actions of humans. If we purify ourselves, we will be in harmony with this cycle of purification in nature. If not, we will be in conflict and in strife with nature. This is not a doomsday prophecy, nor is it a prediction of punishment or reward. It is a prophecy of accountability and of consequences for committed actions.

This prophecy is one of the reasons why the medicine ways of many tribes are being shared openly and why information long kept secret is now released. It is one of the reasons why I am now able to write about and make available information that was previously kept confined to closed circles. Once this information is shared with a good heart, the responsibility for its use or abuse is placed on the recipients. Now is a time when people of all tribes and of all races are coming together and sharing ceremonies of purification, healing, and self-realization, for self-realization is purification. Anglo doctors and lawyers, rabbis, ministers and professors, housewives and their children, of all ethnic backgrounds, religions, and races are participating in sweat ceremonies and preparing for vision quests. Folks are taking sincere steps to reconcile themselves with nature and to seek true religion in God communion.

Purification is neither self-righteous nor a holier-than-thou attitude. It is identifying our ambiguous relationships and our ambivalent attitudes; cleansing our thoughts, feelings, and behavior; making some decisions; choosing some directions. It is new growth—cleansing, shedding, release, renewal. The adversary is most often within ourselves in addictions, ignorance, and illusion. We fall under the spell of power instead of the liberation of true self-realization and awareness. Purification is a distillation of emotion, so that negative and destructive thoughts, feelings, and actions are cleared away. To purify is to concentrate, to compact, and to center the positive, the constructive, and the harmonious.

Purification is overcoming alienation from nature and anchoring in its Source, the Creator. This is not a matter of being religious in a new belief system. It is a matter of getting the distractions out of our lives— whether harmful food, drugs, attitudes, or personal relationships—anything that interferes with our communion with nature and the Great Spirit and with our personal self-realization. True coexistence is peace and harmony developed and maintained among existing differences; coexistence is not trying to eliminate these differences by manipulation nor by forcibly imposing cultural or religious values on others.

Purification is sensitizing our body, mind, and spirit toward new perceptions. Through purification, we begin to see, hear, and feel things we never knew existed because our senses were bombarded and our intuitive wisdom encrusted with layers of negative habits and self-destructive ideas.

Purification is not the absence of fear; it is experiencing fear yet not being intimidated by it. Years ago, a warrior society brother, James Bluewolf, and I were walking down a path at sunrise in the Mission Mountains in western Montana. A large female grizzly bear came walking down the same path toward us. When she saw us, she stood up on her hind legs and looked down at us, raising one of her front paws. My totem and spirit guide is the grizzly. I am one with the grizzly. I raised my right hand in peace and spoke, "I am the grizzly." I greeted her as a relative, not as a predator. She turned and ran away on all fours. She experienced fear; I experienced fear; yet neither of us was intimidated by fear. I was in her territory, and we momentarily shared the same path.

It takes a pure, stable mind to enter the untamed wilderness in peace. One develops, not a cockiness lacking all fear, but rather a reverent innocence. Animals, plants, and minerals sense this purity of innocence. We need to purify ourselves if we are to commune with nature and its Creator and to elicit their responses to us. We must be prepared to accept the forces of nature in alliance.

Many of us feel that the fun and pleasure of life is all over when we think of purity and the spiritual path. I have had adolescents tell me they will embrace the spiritual path when they get older, after they live life and "sow their seeds." This is part of the bondage and spell of the "great delusion," as I call it. It is linear thinking, not circular. It is the great coyote tricking us. But the coyote also tricks us into learning in spite of our arrogance and stubbornness. When I challenged my grandmother into teaching me a ceremony so that I could prove it nothing more than cultural enjoyment, she used coyote medicine with me. She prepared me for my vision quest, which turned me around. My life has never been the same since. My whole life is now a sustained vision quest.

The most powerful and effective tools of purification that I know of are not finding one's medicine person or guru (although such discoveries may be a blessing), but tools of individual prayer and fasting. We mistakenly view prayer as trying to placate some faraway mystical God in awe, or of seeking the supernatural only when in trouble or need. We further incorrectly view fasting as self-sacrifice or self-punishment. Originally, self-sacrifice meant to sanctify, to

make sacred. In fasting, we make our bodies more sacred, fitter vehicles for divine communion. Bodily
practice strengthens the spirit. Self-discipline is a duty
to the self and develops individual dynamic will-
power. It sets the pace for the unfolding of one's
medicine power.

Fasting is a cleansing of impurities. It is periodic
renewal. There are "fasts" from speaking, from speaking certain words, from certain thoughts, and from
behaviors. There are also "food fasts" or temporary
abstinences from certain foods. There are abstinences
from participating in sexual activity. All such fasts
require power and develop power. In any fasting, we
are controlling or "steering" our natural appetites,
perhaps to lessen a struggle occurring in our nature.
Sometimes we may have to dry up the springs of our
passions that may be warring against the soul, or cool
the flame of our blood, or render our mind more capable for spiritual perceptions. The time spent away
from participating in that which we are fasting from
is redirected to spiritual activity and exercises. It can
be a time of joy.

In fasting, we bear witness to the fact that our spirit
is not chained to our body, that it can fly and temporarily release the weight and burden of the body. We
become more than the body. Fasting is big medicine,
especially when coupled with prayer. Healers bring
about intercessory healings of the very sick through
prayer and fasting. Seekers receive visions while praying and fasting. Many times in my life when I approached a medicine person with a problem, his
response was, "Go out alone and pray. Don't eat while
you're doing this." Today when some folks call or
write to me regarding a need, I guide them back to
themselves in prayer and fasting. Sometimes I pray

and fast with them. It is often crucial to seek the source of our pain or problem before determining a solution or plan of action to remedy it.

Prayer is beautiful. Prayer is power. It too is big medicine. There are several types of prayer, such as devotional and intercessory. Prayer involves listening as well as speaking. Often, our times spent in prayer involves only "speaking to" instead of remaining in contemplative silence, solitude, and in stillness to listen. Valuable guidance and direction can be received in contemplative prayer. Medicine people, shamans, and healers may be out for hours or days waiting and seeking guidance in prayer. The power of prayer is too often overlooked; it is a valuable resource and working tool that seems to have been shelved in our religious attics. Every prayer is answered. It may not be the answer we seek or expect, but it is answered. A friend will tell me, "I've been praying about this job and I didn't get it. My prayer wasn't answered." I tell him his prayer was answered; the answer was no. I suggest he set up a Medicine Wheel and examine the possible gain and apparent loss of this potential job in the light and perspective of the four directions.

Some spiritual groups today have established a worldwide circle of prayer. On given days at specific times, folks worldwide are praying simultaneously to counteract the negativity in the world. Some native clans and societies do this during the new and full moons, during eclipses, and at sunrise and sunset, to harmonize their individual prayer power with these times of power in nature. Some healings and ceremonies are performed only during certain lunar or solar phases. Traditionally, most Plains Indian sun dances occurred during the full moon.

It is most important to tune our mind and will in prayer to the divine consciousness of the Great Spirit. In prayer, we form a relationship and a connection with Source, the Great Spirit. All creation is a visible manifestation of the presence of the Great Spirit, the breath of God made visible. Establishing and sustaining a relationship and a connection with the spirit power in nature and with the Source of all power is the beginning stage in the making of medicine. True prayer is based on precise laws that govern nature. It is an understanding of these natural laws and an application of the forces of creation. Prayer is also channeling the power of the Great Spirit. True prayer is one of the most beautiful experiences in life. It can be a conversation with God within (your higher self) or a communication with the infinite, omnipresent wisdom of the Great Spirit. I encourage all seekers on the spiritual path to use and develop prayer and fasting as tools of purification and power. We are our own priests and priestesses. Only through us can the world be purified.

Epilogue:
The Leaves Are Falling

As I pray today, I look around me and see the leaves dropping from the trees. They have all fully turned color this crisp blue-sky sunny morning in northern New Mexico, and now they are being released from their branches by the winds of change. They don't crash directly to the ground; they dance gently in graceful descent to earth, to merge with water and soil to form a mulch for new growth.

The fullness of summer's growth has matured, but the completion of summer is a beginning, the beginning of autumn. So, too, the writing of this book is both a completion and a beginning. I will shed and release the leaves of previous seasons in the autumn of my life, for in the completion of this book, my Red Road commitment has been sealed. I will shed and release, but I will also absorb and grow. New buds of fresh realization will emerge at the completion of this creative movement. Finishing will be a new beginning—for the writer as well as for the reader of this book. This is the truth of circular time.

Writing this book is also a prayer. It is my intention for it to be a living prayer. I am accountable for the experiences and visions recorded in words here.

In accepting new knowledge, the reader becomes responsible and accountable for reflecting, for acting on it or not. My deepest hope is that this book sets a tone for inquiry. It is intended as a field guide and a map; it is not the territory. Try to experience and nourish the spirit of Red Road teachings of earth and sky. This goes beyond learning about them. First understand yourself and strive for harmony with nature before making a commitment to a teacher or to a teaching. Teachers are guides for new territory and sometimes consultants for familiar territory. But a time arrives when one must explore and travel alone.

Although there are things in my life that I will shed and release, I also look forward to the forthcoming experiences of winter renewal, of the new additions from the promise of spring's new growth, and to the future flourishings of the summers in my life. For every loss there is a gain, for every gain, a loss. The leaves are shed to make room for new buds which will yield fresh leaves. In a continuing renewal, the leaves and the tree fertilize earth and refresh life.

My hope and prayer is that the knowledge, experiences, dreams, and visions that I have shared will help you make your values and ideas more real in the seasons of your life. May your dreams and highest goals be manifested in your actions and behavior. May your talk be your walk and your breath of spirit be visible to others. This book is my prayer to refresh you and to make my breath visible to you.

QUEST BOOKS
are published by
The Theosophical Society in America,
Wheaton, Illinois 60189-0270,
a branch of a world organization
dedicated to the promotion of brotherhood and
the encouragement of the study of religion,
philosophy, and science, to the end that man may
better understand himself and his place in
the universe. The Society stands for complete
freedom of individual search and belief.
In the Classics Series well-known
theosophical works are made
available in popular editions.